'We see nothing truly till we understand it.'

John Constable

HAMPSTEAD
HEATH

ISBN 0 9503656 5 3

First published 1984
Printed in Hong Kong by
South China Printing Co.
Typeset by Phoenix Photosetting, Chatham

Published by
Historical Publications Ltd
54 Station Road
New Barnet, Herts.
(Telephone: 607 1628)

HAMPSTEAD HEATH

ALAN FARMER

HISTORICAL PUBLICATIONS

ACKNOWLEDGEMENTS

In writing this book I have received generous assistance from many people, and I owe special debts to Malcolm Holmes and the staff of the Local History Library, London Borough of Camden; to the staff of the Iveagh Bequest, Kenwood; to Christopher Ikin and David Sullivan who read the typescript and made many helpful comments; and not least to my publisher and editor, John Richardson.

THE ILLUSTRATIONS

Illustrations listed below have been reproduced with the kind permission of:

Illustrated London News Picture Library:
67, 77

Fitzwilliam Museum, Cambridge:
32

Museum of London:
78

Victoria and Albert Museum:
34

Guildhall Library, City of London:
42

National Portrait Gallery:
1, 22, 76, 82

Iveagh Bequest, Kenwood:
23, 26, 83

Greater London Council Photographic Library:
75

Bury Art Gallery:
33

London Transport:
81

Routledge and Kegan Paul:
37

Woodmansterne Publications:
52

Lady Maryon Wilson:
36

Bryan Senior:
60

London Borough of Camden:
3, 5, 7, 8, 9, 10, 11, 14, 18, 24, 30, 31, 38, 39, 40, 41, 43, 49, 50, 54, 58, 59, 61, 63, 64, 65, 66, 68, 69, 70, 71, 72, 79, 84, 90, 92, 93, 95, 96 and cover illustration

The maps on pp. 6, 40, 49, 105, 142, 145, 152 and 160 are based upon the Ordnance Survey 6" to the mile map, with the permission of the Controller of Her Majesty's Stationery Office, Crown copyright reserved.

The Cover illustration is of Wyldes Farm by G. Barnard, 1830.

CONTENTS

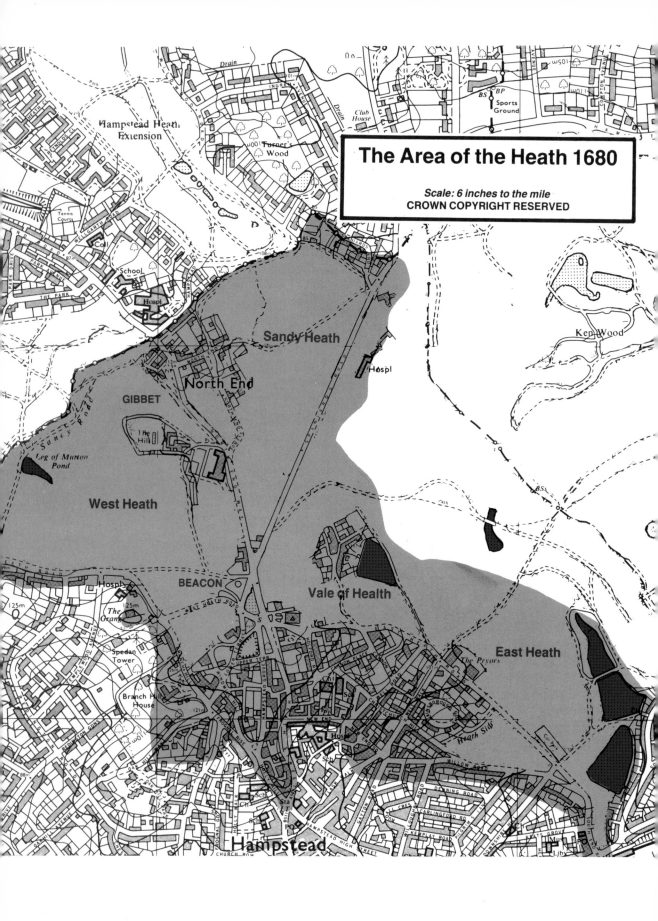

The Area of the Heath 1680

Scale: 6 inches to the mile
CROWN COPYRIGHT RESERVED

CHAPTER ONE
The Village Common

The first map of Hampstead Heath was made by an unknown surveyor in 1680, but this early heath was very different from the one we know today. It was the village common of Hampstead, used as a rough grazing ground for livestock, and it covered only the western part of the present Heath. During the eighteenth century the village of Hampstead expanded and steadily encroached on the Heath. When it became public property in 1871 the Heath had been reduced to some 220 acres, but since then it has been extended by a series of successful campaigns: Parliament Hill was added in 1889, Golders Hill Park in 1898, the Heath Extension in 1907 and Kenwood in 1924–8.

Today the Heath covers over 800 acres of woods and ponds, hills and valleys, meadows and parks. The most remarkable feature is the variety of the landscape. While the original Heath was a sandy common covered with heather and gorse, Parliament Hill and the Heath Extension were good farmland and still reveal a typical pattern of fields and hedges. Kenwood and Golders Hill Park, on the other hand, were landscaped in the eighteenth century as the parks of Georgian mansions. This rich and varied landscape was created by man over many centuries, and the Heath today is a patchwork of history.

Like most of the heaths and moors of Britain, Hampstead Heath was once covered by the forest which gradually spread over the country when the ice retreated after the last Ice Age. In this great forest our ancestors lived a nomadic life, moving from one camp-site to another as they hunted animals and gathered plants for food. Ten years ago the finding of some flints on the West Heath led to the discovery of one of their camp-sites near the Leg of Mutton Pond. A full excavation was carried out and hundreds of flint implements were found, together with an axe, and the postholes of primitive shelters. This Mesolithic site, which dates from between 8000 and 6000 BC, was probably used for several hundred years by nomadic hunting groups who returned to it from time to time.

The first clearings in the forest were made by the Neolithic immigrants who arrived in Britain from the Continent in about 5000 BC. These people were primitive farmers who made clearings for their crops and animals. It has been established by pollen analysis that one of their settlements was made on the sandy soil of the West Heath, and for thousands of years this land was used for growing crops and pasturing cattle. Then, probably in the Iron Age, crop cultivation ceased and it became only a grazing ground for livestock. This is the origin of the Heath.

Hampstead Heath is therefore a very ancient landscape and its early inhabitants must have left burial mounds and earthworks, as they did on other old heaths near London such as Blackheath and Wimbledon Common. Unfortunately little or nothing remains of these prehistoric sites. There is said to have been an earthwork on the crown of the Heath near Jack Straw's Castle, which may possibly have been the 'castle' from which the inn took its name, but it has now been obliterated. The mound on Parliament Hill known as 'Boadicea's Grave' may perhaps be a burial mound (although it is certainly not Boadicea's), but there is considerable doubt about this as we shall see later.

In medieval times Hampstead was a small upland village on the road from London to St Albans. It had a single thoroughfare, Kingswell Street, where the present High Street runs. The village church stood where St John's parish church is today, and nearby on Mount Vernon was the windmill for the manor. Hampstead manor belonged to the abbot and monks of Westminster Abbey, one of the wealthiest monasteries in England, and the manor house or grange stood at the top of Frognal Lane. South and west of the grange, near the present Finchley Road, stretched the demesne land belonging to Westminster Abbey, the best farmland in the manor.

To the north and east lay the village common, Hampstead Heath. At this time, and indeed up to the end of the eighteenth century, village commons (including the common woods) were a vital part of the English rural economy; the soil belonged to the lord of the manor but the commoners had legal rights over the land. The most important of these were the right to graze animals (common of pasture), the right to gather wood for fuel, house repairs and fencing (common of estovers), and the right to dig turf for fuel and roofing (common of turbary).

The first written record of the Heath occurs in 1312, when a valuation of the manor makes a brief mention of a 'certain heath' of which the brushwood was worth two shillings a year to the lord of the manor.[1] Much more valuable were the six manor woods – Northwode, Notehirst, Sheppbrighull, Wytebirche, Brockhole and Tymberhurst. We know the location of two of them from early documents: Northwode lay to the north of Oak Hill Park and Wytebirche stretched from north to south across what is now the middle of the Heath, separating the East Heath from Kenwood.

Gerard's Heath

What did Hampstead Heath look like in these early times? John Gerard, the Elizabethan herbalist, had a house in Holborn and used to make plant-hunting expeditions into the countryside round London. The heath and woods of Hampstead were his favourite hunting ground, and in his *Herball*[2] he gives us the earliest description of their appearance.

The upper heath was a rough common covered with heather, gorse and broom. 'Heath groweth upon dry mountaines which are hungry and barren', wrote Gerard, 'as upon Hampstead Heath neere London, where all the sorts do grow, except that with the white floures, and that which beareth

1. John Gerard.

berries.' 'Butcher's broom', he wrote, 'groweth plentifully in most places in England upon rough and barren grounds, especially upon Hampsted heath.' He found wild cow-wheat growing 'among the Iuniper bushes and bilberry bushes in all the parts of the said heath', and lilies-of-the-valley grew there in 'great abundance'. Orchids grew in North End and Highgate: 'That kinde which resembleth the white Butter-fly groweth upon the declining of the hill at the north end of Hampsted heath, neere unto a small cottage there in the way side, as yee go from London to Henden a village thereby. It groweth in the fields adioyning to the pound or pinnefold without the gate, at the Village called High-gate, neere London.'

There were several bogs and swampy valleys on the Heath: 'Cotton grasse groweth upon bogs and such like moorish places, and is to be seen upon the

2. Map of Kent showing the Tudor invasion warning beacons (W. Lambarde, 1576).

bogs on Hampsted heath.' Water fern 'groweth in the midst of a bog at the further end of Hampsted heath from London, at the bottom of a hill adioyning to a small cottage'.

In describing where he found some of the plants, Gerard makes valuable references to local landmarks. He found kidney vetch 'growing upon Hampstead Heath neere London, right against the Beacon, upon the right hand as you go from London, neere unto a gravell pit'. This beacon, which stood for many years on the summit of the Heath near Whitestone Pond, was an important link in the system of fire beacons built in Elizabeth's reign to give warning of invasion. William Lambarde published a map of the network of beacons in Kent (Illustration 2) showing that a warning from any part of the county had to be relayed through Shooters Hill and from there to Hampstead.[3] No doubt the system was used at the time of the Armada.

Another of the early botanists, and a much better one than Gerard, was Thomas Johnson who edited the second edition of the *Herball*. Johnson was a leading member of the Society of Apothecaries, which was in the habit of going on botanical rambles near London, and on 1 August 1629 he and nine companions made an expedition to Hampstead Heath. Johnson's description of the expedition (in Latin) is the first published account of a botanical excursion in the London area.[4]

Many other botanists followed in the steps of Gerard and Johnson. With its heathland, woods and bogs, and its north- and south-facing slopes, Hampstead Heath offered the botanist an exceptionally wide variety of plants until the late nineteenth century. Indeed the Heath holds a special place in the history of botany; there are few areas of its size anywhere in the world where the flora is better documented.

3. 'The Fleet River near Hampstead' (E. Evans, 1854). A view from the meadows where Fleet Road was later made, with Christ Church on the skyline.

Reservoirs for London

The Tudor period saw the first attempt to develop the springs on Hampstead Heath as one of the sources of London's water supply.

The dominating physical feature of the Heath is·the Hampstead-Highgate

11

ridge, a crescent of high ground rising at either end to form the twin crests of Hampstead and Highgate. The upper part of the ridge consists of Bagshot Sand, and this is surrounded by a belt of sandy clay (the Claygate Beds) which forms the layer below the sand; below this again lies the London Clay. Rainwater percolates through the sand until it reaches the impermeable clay, then oozes out to the surface of the hill at the junction of the sand and clay, forming springs and marshy ground which are the sources of the many streams on the Heath.

South of the Hampstead-Highgate ridge there are two major streams, separated by Parliament Hill. The western or Hampstead brook has its source near the Vale of Health and flows through the Hampstead Ponds, while the eastern or Highgate brook rises near Kenwood and flows through the Highgate Ponds. The two streams meet just north of Camden Town to form the Fleet River, which flows through London to join the Thames at

4. 'A view of Hampstead from the Pond' (J. B. Chatelain, 1745), looking across the lowest pond (later filled in) with the houses of Pond Street in the background.

Blackfriars. Originally the two streams and the river were above ground but today the Fleet flows underground, one of the lost rivers of London,[5] and the two brooks can only be seen above ground on the Heath.[6]

In Tudor times the problem of London's water supply was becoming acute and in 1544 the City Corporation decided to tap the springs outside the City; they obtained an Act of Parliament, the London Conduit Act, to give them the necessary powers. Its preamble describes with some pride the City Corporation's search for new sources of water supply:

Sir William Bowyer Knyght nowe Mayre of the saide Citie, intending and pondering the same necessite, muche willing to helpe and releve the saide Citie and Suburbes with new fountaynes and fresh sprynges for the comoditie of the Kinges said subjects, calling to him as well dyvers grave and expert parsones of his bretherne and other of the cominaltie of the saide Citie, as other parsones in and abóutes the conveyance of Water well experimented, hath not oonly by dylygent

13

serche and exploracion found out dyvers great and plentifull springes at Hampstede Hethe, Marybon, Hakkney, Muswell Hill, and dyvers places within fyve miles of the said Citie, very mete, propice, and convenyent to be brought and conveyed to the same, but also hath labored studied and devysed the conveaunce therof by conduytes vautes and pypes to the saide Citie, and otherwise to his great travayle labor and payne.

After all this, it is rather an anti-climax to find that nothing was done to bring water from Hampstead Heath for another forty-five years. Finally, in 1589, the City Corporation drew up a scheme for 'drawing diverse springes about Hampsted heath into one head and course' with the dual purpose of supplying fresh water to the City and scouring the Fleet river which was clogged with refuse. John Gerard was one of the party which came to view the Hampstead springs; he recorded the occasion in the *Herball* under the heading 'Broad Leaved Hedge Hyssope':

I found it growing upon the bog or marrish ground at the further end of Hampstead heath, and upon the same heath towards London, neere unto the head of the springs that were digged for water to be conveied to London, 1590, attempted by that carefull citizen Iohn Hart Knight, Lord Major of the City of London: at which time my selfe was in his Lordships company, and viewing for my pleasure the same goodly springs, I found the said plant, not heretofore remembred.

We do not know what kind of waterworks were made on the Heath at this time. All we know is that the scheme failed to scour the Fleet river which according to John Stow, the Elizabethan historian of London, became 'woorse cloyed and choken, than ever it was before'.

5. Highgate Ponds (T. Hastings c.1825).

SIC VOS NON VOBIS

6. William Paterson.

A hundred years elapsed before the springs on the Heath were developed further. This time the promoter was William Paterson, an enterprising Scotsman who came to London and prospered in the West Indies trade. He is generally known as the founder of the Bank of England, and was indeed the leading figure in the group which drew up the scheme for the Bank; he also took the lead in the disastrous scheme to plant a Scottish colony in Darien on the Panama isthmus.

In 1692 the City Corporation leased the springs on Hampstead Heath to Paterson and his partners, who formed the Hampstead Water Company. The Company gradually made the string of reservoirs known as the Hampstead Ponds; a survey of the manor in 1703–4[7] shows two ponds and two more were made later. The lowest pond lay at the foot of Keats Grove until 1892 when it was filled in. Another series of six reservoirs, the Highgate Ponds, was made by damming the eastern stream on the other side of Parliament Hill.

The Hampstead system of reservoirs was later extended by adding the Vale of Health Pond in 1777. The Hampstead Water Company, also known as the Society of Hampstead Aqueducts, supplied water to a large part of north London through wooden pipes made of bored elm trunks; it was eventually taken over by the New River Company in 1859.

The Heath in 1680

In 1889 an early map of the Heath came to light in an old manuscript volume in a Cambridge bookshop which was later bought by the Hampstead Vestry.[8] The volume has no title page or author's name but is inscribed on the back 'Trigonometry H.O. 1680'; it contains treatises on various subjects including Fortification, Trigonometry and Logarithms. The pages dealing with the Heath are headed:

The Feild Booke
Aprill the 25th 1680 Measured Hamsted Heath
begining at Pond Street and goeing North west.

The 'Feild Booke' then gives all the stations, angles and distances noted in the survey, together with an outline plan of the Heath on a scale of 20 inches to the mile. The most interesting feature is the Heath's southern boundary (see map on p. 6). This ran, to use modern street names, down Holly Hill, up Heath Street, along New End past the site of the hospital, and then turned right down the lower part of New End. From there it followed the old stream which ran south of Willow Road, and then turned south to Pond Street.

The Heath therefore covered a large part of what is now Hampstead Village, including Upper and Lower Terrace, Windmill Hill, Elm Row, Hampstead Square, Christchurch Hill, Well Walk and Willow Road. The district we know as New End is marked on the map as 'the end of ye town'. But the Heath did not include Kenwood, Parliament Hill, Golders Hill Park or the Heath Extension, and covered only 337 acres in all.

The map shows various local landmarks such as 'the Beacon Stafe' near Whitestone Pond and 'ye mill' on Mount Vernon. This was one of two windmills which stood on Hampstead Hill; the other was on the site now occupied by New Grove House in Hampstead Grove. These two mills can be clearly seen on the skyline in the panoramic views of London made by C. J. Visscher and Wenceslaus Hollar in the seventeenth century. There was also a windmill at North End, and there may have been another on Parliament Hill.

Another landmark was the well-known gibbet which stood near North End Way, from which (when the map was made) the body of Francis Jackson the highwayman was hanging in chains. Jackson was the leader of a gang who committed a series of robberies in 1674. After holding up two coaches near Staines they made their escape to Harrow, where they were met by fifty men with guns and pitchforks; they escaped again and rode on to Kilburn, Hendon and Hampstead Heath, where another party of armed men was waiting for them. In a fierce battle Jackson killed one of the Hampstead party before they were taken; the gang was sentenced to death

7. 'The Hollow Elme of Hampstead' (after W. Hollar, 1653).

and hanged.

When highwaymen were convicted of murder and hanged, it was the practice for their bodies to be gibbeted near the scene of the crime, the corpses being hung in an iron framework and left there for years as a grisly warning. Jackson's body was exhibited on the left of the road from Jack Straw's Castle to North End. The gibbet stood between two trees, the Gibbet Elms, one of which survived until 1907 when it was blown down in a gale, and the district was known for many years as Gibbet Hill.

This was the heyday of highwaymen and footpads who menaced all the heaths and commons round London. Hampstead Heath had its full share of armed robberies, although it was not as dangerous as Hounslow Heath and Finchley Common which were crossed by major roads. Many attacks which took place on the Heath, sometimes ending in murder, are recorded in the London newspapers of the eighteenth century. According to local legend Dick Turpin was associated with the Heath and used the Spaniards Inn; the landlord is said to have given him spare keys to the stables and the tollgate so that he could make a quick escape if necessary. But like most of the Turpin legends this is probably apocryphal.

Another well-known landmark in the seventeenth century was the 'Hollow Elme Tree of Hampstead' which stood on the Heath. This great tree, Hampstead's first tourist attraction, was twenty-eight feet in girth and had a hollow trunk containing a winding staircase with forty-two steps. At the top, thirty-three feet above ground, was a turret which could hold six

(Overleaf)
8. Vale of Health Pond (T. Stowers, 1796).

17

people seated and fourteen standing. The tree must have stood near the summit of the Heath, since from the turret it was possible to see Harrow, Acton, Richmond, Windsor Castle and the ships on the Thames. A broadsheet of 1653 gives a description of this elm, with an engraving by Hollar, and some verses in which the poet asks the tree:

> What shall I call thee, who, so great and high,
> Present'st thyself unto my wond'ring eye?
> Thou traveller's fence and guide! the interlude
> O' th' ranting storms, and giant of the wood![9]

[1] J. Kennedy: *The Manor and Parish Church of Hampstead* (1906).

[2] John Gerard: *The Herball, or General Historie of Plantes* (1597).

[3] William Lambarde: *The Perambulation of Kent* (1576).

[4] Thomas Johnson: *Botanical Journeys in Kent and Hampstead*, edited by J. S. Gilmour (1972).

[5] Nicholas Barton: *The Lost Rivers of London* (1962).

[6] The Hampstead stream can be seen below the Viaduct Pond, and the Highgate stream near the sham bridge at Kenwood.

[7] J. J. Park: *The Topography and Natural History of Hampstead* (1814).

[8] It is now in the Local History Collection, Swiss Cottage Library.

[9] J. J. Park, op. cit.

CHAPTER TWO
The Eighteenth Century

Early in the eighteenth century the mineral springs of Hampstead were developed and the village grew into a small town. Daniel Defoe gives a graphic description of the change:

> Hampstead indeed is risen from a little Country Village, to a City, not upon the Credit only of the Waters, Though 'tis apparent, its growing Greatness began there; but Company increasing gradually and the People liking both the Place and the Diversions together; it grew suddenly Populous, and the Concourse of People was Incredible. This consequently raised the Rate of Lodgings, and that increased Buildings, till the Town grew up from a little Village, to a Magnitude equal to some Cities; nor could the uneven Surface, inconvenient for Building, uncompact, and unpleasant, check the humour of the Town, for even on the very steep of the Hill, where there's no walking Twenty Yards together, without Tugging up a Hill, or Straddling down a Hill, yet 'tis all one, the Buildings encreased to that degree, that the Town almost spreads the whole side of the Hill.
>
> On the Top of the Hill, indeed, there is a very pleasant Plain, called the Heath, which on the very Summit is a Plain of about a Mile every way; and in good Weather 'tis pleasant Airing upon it, and some of the Streets are extended so far, as that they begin to build even on the highest part of the Hill. But it must be confest, 'tis so near to Heaven, that I dare not say it can be a proper Situation for any but a race of mountaineers, whose lungs had been used to a rarify'd air.[1]

In the seventeenth century City merchants were already finding Hampstead a pleasant place in which to build their country houses, but the real impetus to expansion came from the mineral springs. At this time it was becoming fashionable to take the waters, and over a hundred mineral springs were discovered and promoted in different parts of England. The well at Hampstead is first recorded in the mid-seventeenth century, and in 1697 that intrepid traveller Celia Fiennes wrote of 'a quick spring as Tunbridg or the Spaw or Hamsted waters, which have all fine stone basons in which you see the springs bubble up.'[2]

But Hampstead Wells really dates from 1698 when the Hon. Susanna Noel, mother of the young Earl of Gainsborough who was lord of the manor, granted six acres of Hampstead Heath including 'the well of medicinal waters' to trustees for the benefit of the poor of Hampstead.[3] This stretch of boggy heath lay on both sides of what is now Well Walk. The trustees leased part of the land to a speculator, John Duffield, who put up the Great Room, a large building on the south side of Well Walk combining a pump room and assembly hall. Concerts and dancing attracted the fashionable crowds, while lodging houses and a tavern sprang up in the surrounding district, which became known as New End. For a few years

(Overleaf)
9. 'View of Hampstead from Primrose Hill' (Royce, 1775).

21

10. *'A north view of the Cities of London and Westminster with part of Highgate. Taken from Hampstead Heath, near the Spaniards.' (George Robertson, 1780)*

Hampstead was a fashionable spa, but its nearness to London attracted gamblers and card sharpers and it soon acquired a bad reputation.

A new start was made in the 1730s when John Soame, a local doctor, published a book on the Wells in which he gives an enthusiastic description of Hampstead:

> Here it is, that you draw in a pure and balmy Air, with the Heavens clear and serene above you, in that Season of the Year that the great and populous City of *London* (from which it is distant not above four Miles) is cover'd with Fogs, Smoaks, and other thick Darkness, being frequently oblig'd to burn Candles in the middle of the Day; while we are here bless'd with the benign and comfortable Rays of a glorious Sun, breathing a free and wholesome Air without the noisome Smell of stinking Fogs, or other malignant Fumes and Vapours, too, too common in large Cities.[4]

This was the beginning of the second phase of Hampstead Wells, in which it gradually acquired a fresh lease of popularity, a more respectable clientèle and a better reputation.

The Heath Discovered

As Hampstead grew in size and popularity the fame of the Heath grew with it. The visitors to the spa soon discovered its pleasures and it was promoted by John Soame as one of the main attractions of Hampstead Wells:

> *Hampstead* Heath being chiefly Gravel and Sand, is always dry and pleasant, unless it be in excessive and long Rains; yet then in a few Days time of dry Weather, you may walk very well, the water soon running off. This Heath also is famous for the vast number of useful Plants that grow all over it . . . The Apothecaries Company very seldom miss coming to *Hampstead* every Spring, and here have their Herbarising Feast; and I have heard them often say, that they have found a greater Variety of curious and useful Plants, near and about *Hampstead*, than in any other Place.[5]

Several places of entertainment were established on the edge of the Heath to cater for the influx of visitors. One of the earliest was Mother Huff's, a tavern which stood near Spaniards Road where The Elms is today. Not far away was the Spaniards Inn, probably named after Francis Porero who held the licence in 1721.[6] Some years later another landlord, William Staples, made the Spaniards pleasure garden which had among its attractions 'many curious figures, depicted with pebble stones of various colours'.[7] There was also a mount from which, it was claimed, Hanslop Steeple near Northampton could be seen. Another pleasure garden, New Georgia, was in Turner's Wood near the present Wildwood Road.

At the other end of Spaniards Road, near Jack Straw's Castle, there was a 'horse-course' on the West Heath where the Hampstead races were popular in the 1730s and 1740s until they were prohibited by the magistrates. Near the present Hampstead Grove stood a large green and an old village tree under which George Whitefield preached in 1739, urging his audience to turn their minds away from the horse-course to the spiritual race. His diary records that 'most were attentive, but some mocked'.

There were several walks and avenues around the Heath. One of these was Judges' Walk, then called Prospect Walk, which was more impressive

11. *'The South View of the Spaniards near Hampstead' (J. B. Chatelain, 1750), showing the Spaniards Pleasure Garden.*

25

12. Heath House with
Whitestone Pond in the
foreground (J. Ramsey,
1755).

13. Judges' Walk
(G. Stanfield, c.1850).

*14. The Village Tree
(T. Hastings, 1826).*

than it is now, with three rows of trees making a fine double avenue. Mrs Barbauld, the author and poetess, wrote of Hampstead in 1787 that 'the mall of the place, a kind of terrace, which they call Prospect Walk, commands a most extensive and varied view over Middlesex and Berkshire, in which is included, besides many inferior places, the majestic Windsor and lofty Harrow'.[8]

Judges' Walk is clearly shown on John Rocque's Plan of London in 1745 (Illustration 15). This authoritative publication, based on a careful survey of London and its suburbs, gives us the first detailed map of the area. The 'horse-course' on the West Heath can be distinguished, and the New Georgia pleasure garden is also shown. The Highgate Ponds can be seen although they are confusingly marked Hampstead Ponds. Only two of the real Hampstead Ponds are shown; two more were evidently made soon after, since four ponds appear in a map of the manor made in 1762.

The Manor Court

From the legal point of view Hampstead Heath was a common belonging to the manor of Hampstead, and before going any further we must consider what this meant in practice.

As mentioned earlier, the lord of the manor was legal owner of the soil but the copyhold tenants (or copyholders) had common rights including the freedom to pasture their animals. The conflict between these two parties runs through the history of the Heath in the eighteenth and nineteenth centuries.

For five-and-a-half centuries the lord of the manor was the Abbot of Westminster, but the dissolution of the monasteries ended monastic rule in Hampstead. In 1551 Edward VI gave the manor to his favourite, Sir Thomas Wroth, whose family held it until 1620. It was then sold to Sir Baptist Hickes, a rich City merchant whose daughter's descendants became the Earls of Gainsborough. The third Earl sold it in 1707 to Sir William Langhorne, a wealthy East India Company merchant, from whom it descended to his cousins, the Maryon family.

Since none of the lords of the manor lived in Hampstead, the manor was managed by a steward appointed by the lord. The manor court was summoned at Whitsun and Christmas. In medieval times these courts could dispense justice in minor matters but they had lost most of their powers by the eighteenth century. The main responsibilities of Hampstead's manor court were to deal with grants and transfers of copyholds and supervise the Heath. The lord was represented by the steward, who presided, and the copyholders by a jury known as the homage.

Each manor had its own customs, and one of Hampstead's allowed the lord, with the consent of the homage, to make grants of the 'waste of the manor' (which consisted mainly of the Heath) to existing copyholders. A copyholder who wanted such a grant made his application to the court. If lord and homage agreed an 'entry fine' was paid to the lord and the grant was recorded in the Court Rolls – the records of the manor court. The copyholder thus held his land 'by copy of court roll' – hence the term copyholder.

These 'grants of the waste' provided the building plots required by the expanding village. In all 442 grants were made between 1680 and 1866, for about 82 acres of land in total.[9] The bulk of these were on the Heath and this is where most of Georgian Hampstead was built. To the south and west of the village lay private farmland which was not available for building, but the Heath was inferior land which could be acquired more cheaply. So the

(Facing Page)
15. Section of Rocque's Map of London (1745).

Georgian houses and terraces climbed up the hill and encroached on the Heath, which contracted from 337 acres in 1680 to 225 acres in the middle of the nineteenth century.

The manor court also had to deal with the difficult problem of squatters who built their primitive cottages on the Heath; this was illegal and the cottages were pulled down when the manor was strictly administered. In May 1737, for example, the court laid down that 'all incroachments which shall be made hereafter within this manor and presented at any court shall be pulled down, laid open, removed, and taken away, or the persons making the same shall be otherwise prosecuted, fined, or punished for the same, in such manner as by any law, custom, or usage they may'.

But at some periods the manor administration was laxer and on two occasions it broke down altogether. The first was in 1684 when the steward's house was burnt down and the records of the manor were destroyed. The second breakdown occurred some years later when the lord appointed a new steward but the old one refused to accept his dismissal leading to a long dispute which was eventually referred to the Court of Chancery. On both occasions squatters took advantage of the confusion to build cottages on the Heath; they were later given grants, after making a payment, and allowed to become copyholders.

Hamlets on the Heath

In addition to the expanding village, several outlying hamlets grew up around the Heath, sometimes starting as colonies of squatters. The history of two of these has been studied in detail and they make an interesting contrast.

In the early eighteenth century, during the periods of breakdown mentioned above, several squatters erected cottages on the land just to the north of Jack Straw's Castle, and were later allowed to become copyholders.[10] The parish almshouses and the village pound were also part of this little hamlet, which was known by the revealing name of Littleworth. An engraving by J. T. Smith, *Rustic Cottage near Jack Straw's Castle* (Illustration 16), shows what appears to be one of the squatters' cottages at a later date.

But the squatters had chosen a magnificent site near the summit of the Heath and they were gradually eased out by the gentry who purchased their copyholds. Their cottages were replaced by handsome villas, one of which belonged to the beautiful Mrs Crewe, the famous Whig hostess who entertained Fox, Burke and Sheridan. The parish almshouses and the pound were banished to the Vale of Health, and eventually the humble Littleworth became the wealthy hamlet of Heath Brow.

Not far away, where the Vale of Health now stands, was a malarial swamp inhabited by frogs and mosquitoes. In the early eighteenth century the only human inhabitant was Samuel Hatch, a harness-maker with a cottage and a workshop, and the site was known as Hatches or Hatchett's Bottom.[11] But in 1777 the Hampstead Water Company drained the swamp to make their new reservoir, the Vale of Health Pond, and the drained land become available for building. The low-lying situation did not appeal to the

*16. 'Rustic Cottage near
Jack Straw's Castle'
(J. T. Smith, 1797).*

gentry but was considered most suitable for the parish almshouses which
were moved down the hill from Littleworth in 1778. A few months later
Sarah and John Whitethread, apparently squatters, were granted pieces of
land on which they had already built cottages. Several more cottages were
built but at the end of the century Hatches Bottom was still a very small
settlement.

Another hamlet, socially superior to Hatches Bottom, grew up at Heath
End near the Spaniards Inn. The largest house, later known as The Firs, was
built in 1734 by John Turner, a retired merchant. Turner shared the
eighteenth-century passion for landscaping and planted clumps of pines
near his house and avenues extending across the Heath. The hamlet of
North End also expanded in the eighteenth century.

These outlying hamlets were linked by roads across the Heath. One of
these, known as the Sandy Road, ran from the Spaniards to North End and
remained open to vehicles as a public road until the twentieth century.
Another road, from the Spaniards to the Vale of Health, continued in use
until the 1840s when the lord of the manor made a road through his East
Park estate, cutting across the old road and making it unusable. The old
track can still be clearly seen on the Heath, marked by a line of oaks and
beeches running south from the gate of The Elms.

*17. The Vale of Health
(F. J. Sarjent, 1804).*

*18. The old road from
the Spaniards to the
Vale of Health, with
Christ Church spire
behind the trees (J. S.
Whitty, c.1868).*

The Riot of Hampstead Heath

The following entry appears in the manor court rolls for 29 May 1775:

> At this Court Jane Hemett of Charlotte Street in the County of Middlesex spinster prayed to have a grant made to her of a piece or parcel of ground (part of the waste of the said Manor) lying on Hampstead Heath on the West side of the road leading to North End near Mr Havard's house and garden at a place called Gibbett Hill, not exceeding three hundred and twenty rods or two acres in order to erect a house and buildings thereon. And the Homage at the request of the said Jane Hemett have this day viewed the said ground and given their opinion at this Court, that it will be of no detriment for the Lord to make the said Grant to the said Jane Hemett of the said parcel of Waste and they testify their consent to the Lord's making an immediate grant thereof.

Behind this entry lies an interesting story which throws a vivid light on Georgian Hampstead and the people who lived there. It has not been fully told before, although it is mentioned by Park and Barratt in their histories of Hampstead. Jane Hemett was a well-known actress at Covent Garden Theatre whose stage name was Mrs Lessingham. At this time she was 'under the protection' of William Addington, usually referred to as Mr Justice Addington, who was the father of her 3-year-old son Frederick. Addington, who plays an important part in the story, was a versatile man who started his career in the Church; he then transferred to the army and rose to the rank of major but retired after his marriage. He was a close friend of Sir John Fielding, the famous 'blind beak' of Bow Street, who persuaded Addington to become one of his assistant magistrates; after Fielding's death Addington succeeded him as Chief Magistrate at Bow Street and was given a knighthood. He also wrote several plays, and no doubt it was his connection with the theatre that led to his liaison with Mrs Lessingham.

Mrs Lessingham, who had a small house at Golders Green, wanted to build a larger one on the Heath, and Addington found an attractive site on the West Heath near North End Way. To obtain a grant of this land the first step was to approach the lord of the manor of Hampstead. At this date the effective representative of the lord was General Sir Thomas Spencer Wilson, a member of an old Sussex family who had acquired a baronetcy in the reign of Charles II. As a young officer Sir Thomas had fought at the battle of Minden, where his horse was shot from under him, and he later commanded a regiment in the American War of Independence. He also restored the family fortunes, which had fallen to a low ebb, by marrying an heiress, Jane Weller. Jane's mother was a member of the wealthy Maryon family who had inherited large estates from Sir William Langhorne, the East India merchant; these included Charlton House near Greenwich and land in Kent, Essex and Hampstead, together with the lordship of the manor of Hampstead. Jane inherited these estates on her mother's death in 1777 and Sir Thomas became lord of the manor of Hampstead.

Early in 1775 Justice Addington asked Sir Thomas (who was not yet lord of the manor but was evidently acting for his mother-in-law) for a grant of two acres of Hampstead Heath for Mrs Lessingham. This application was unusual in two respects. First, the grant applied for was an exceptionally large one, in fact one of the largest recorded in the Court Rolls. Secondly,

19. Mrs Lessingham.

grants were normally made only to existing copyholders, which Mrs Lessingham was not, although she became one later by acquiring a copyhold cottage during the subsequent dispute. But Addington was a man of influence and Sir Thomas agreed to this unusual grant. A formal application was then made to the manor court on 29 May, but at a further court held on 7 July there was strong disagreement among the copyholders who formed the homage; a minority, led by a builder named Henry White, vigorously opposed the application but the majority approved it and the grant was made.

Mrs Lessingham's builder, Bradley, then started work on the site, but on 12 August a report appeared in the *St James' Chronicle*:

> On Thursday last at Ten in the Morning, a Detachment of Copyholders from Hampstead, led on by their commanding Officers, proceeded to fill up the Fosse and destroy the Lines of Circumvallation which a celebrated theatrical Heroine had drawn round a Part of the Heath, on which she designed to erect her Castle. Having performed this service, they left a Garrison, consisting of Cows, Hogs and Asses, on the Spot; and then marched back in Triumph to their Head Quarters.

On the same day the *Morning Post* printed a rather different account in its report of cases dealt with at Bow Street:

> John Kennedy, a labourer, from Hampstead-heath, was committed to Newgate, for threatening to shoot and otherwise abusing Mr Bradley, a Builder, in Long-acre; it appeared that a lady had obtained a grant from the lord of the manor of Hampstead, of about two acres of ground on the common; and that almost all the Copyholders, except one or two, had signed a proper instrument. The lady

having begun to lay a foundation for building some houses; whatever her labourers did during the day, was demolished at night; a watch being set to discover the perpetrators, Kennedy was found to be one, and swore he was prepared with fire arms, and would shoot the first that opposed him; and to intimidate any from the attempt, discharged several shot.

This was the beginning of a furious argument about the 'riot of Hampstead Heath', filling many columns of the London papers, which took sides for and against Mrs Lessingham. Her opponents said they had been advised by eminent counsel that the grant was illegal because the court on 7 July had not been properly summoned. They denied that there had been a riot on the Heath, and said that Kennedy and Bradley had quarrelled in an alehouse; Kennedy had then been taken to Bow Street, where he had been committed to Newgate – by Justice Addington!

Mrs Lessingham's supporters replied that she was being unfairly treated because she was an actress, which had nothing to do with the case. She had not been shown any favour by the lord of the manor, having paid a considerable sum for the grant, and had been properly admitted by the manor court; if there was any complaint it should be made to the Steward and the homage. As for Henry White, the builder, he was only complaining because Mrs Lessingham had not employed him to build her house.

On 17 August the *St James' Chronicle* extended the attack to Justice Addington:

> The following case is submitted to the opinion of the Gentlemen of the Law:- B steals a Goose from Hampstead heath, and is taken up and carried before Mr Justice A, who commits him to Prison for the Fact. Mr Justice A in the mean Time takes upon him to defend the Proceeding of Mrs C, who as unlawfully has possessed herself of two Acres of the said Heath on which a whole Flock of Geese might have been maintained. Query, Which is the more valuable, the Goose or the Land? and consequently which of the two Culprits is the greater?

20. Heath Lodge (A. R. Quinton, 1910).

Finally, the copyholders opposing Mrs Lessingham announced that they were taking the matter to court. A few weeks later her supporters published a satirical pamphlet in verse entitled *The Hampstead Contest*. A copy of this very rare pamphlet, which has not been reprinted before, has been found in Birmingham Reference Library and is reproduced in the Appendix.

The copyholders' suit against Mrs Lessingham was heard in the Court of Common Pleas a few months later; the result was a victory for the actress, the jury taking the view that the copyholders were not damaged since the land was of no value. This was a serious defeat for the copyholders, but the story has a happy ending. Mrs Lessingham built Heath Lodge, a handsome Georgian house, said to have been designed by James Wyatt, where she spent the rest of her days. The house has since been pulled down but the lovely garden is now open to the public as The Hill Garden; it has changed a good deal since Mrs Lessingham's day but the three towering beeches on the lawn were probably planted in the eighteenth century.

Another dispute flared up in 1780 when Sir Thomas Spencer Wilson questioned the right of the copyholders to dig sand and gravel on the Heath for their own use. The copyholders, again led by Henry White, the builder, brought an action against him which was tried before Lord Mansfield. The verdict was reported in the *Gazetteer and New Daily Advertiser* on 27 February 1781:

> On Friday last a cause in the Court of King's Bench, between Sir Thomas Spencer Wilson, Lord of the Manor of Hampstead, in right of his wife, and the copyholders of the same district, concerning the privilege of digging loam, sand, gravel etc., was determined in favour of the latter, who will continue as usual to open pits and cut turf, in defiance of him and his agents. The verdict of the special jury afforded universal satisfaction to a crowded court: nor should those who are benefitted by this welcome decision forget that their success was, in great measure, owing to the activity and good sense of Mr White, bricklayer, of the place aforesaid, who (to use the language of Gray) 'may be regarded as 'A village Hampden, who with dauntless breast/The little tyrant of his fields withstood.'

Many years later Henry White's son recalled an exchange between his father and Sir Thomas after the verdict. Putting his hand on Henry White's shoulder, Sir Thomas said:

'Well, White, you have beat me.'

'Yes, Sir Thomas, we have and I am glad of it.'

'I don't blame you, I like a man of spirit. I thought it was my right but I find it is not.'

Henry White became a successful builder whose descendants took their place among the Hampstead gentry; his son and grandson were among the leading defenders of the Heath against Sir Thomas' grandson in the nineteenth century.

[1] Daniel Defoe: *A Tour through the Whole Island of Great Britain* (1724).
[2] *The Journeys of Celia Fiennes* (edited by C. Morris, 1949).
[3] G. W. Potter: *Hampstead Wells* (1904).
[4] John Soame: *Hampstead Wells, or Directions for the Drinking of those Waters* (1734).
[5] Ibid.
[6] See p. 159.
[7] J. J. Park, op. cit.
[8] Betsy Rogers: *A Georgian Chronicle* (1958).
[9] Observations for the Hearing, Hoare v. Wilson papers, in the Local History Collection, London Borough of Camden.
[10] *Hampstead & Highgate Express*, 25 May 1979. Article by David Sullivan.
[11] Helen Bentwich: *The Vale of Health* (1968).

CHAPTER THREE
Kenwood

From north to south across the centre of the Heath runs an ancient boundary line marked by parish boundary stones.[1] Starting at the southern limit of the Heath, near the footbridge over the railway from Savernake Road, it runs north-west along the ridge between the East Heath and Parliament Hill. After passing near the western end of the Kenwood woodland, it bears right and enters the Kenwood gardens near the Spaniards.

When the Domesday Survey was made in 1086 this was the boundary between two manors – Hampstead belonging to Westminster Abbey, and Tottenhall or Totehele belonging to St Paul's. It was also a parish boundary and until 1965 it divided the boroughs of Hampstead and St Pancras. Kenwood and Parliament Hill lay to the east of the boundary in the manor of Tottenhall, and in the parish and later borough of St Pancras. They did not become part of Hampstead Heath until 1889 (in the case of Parliament Hill) and 1924–8 (in the case of Kenwood), but they are part of it today and their history is an important part of the story of the Heath.

The earliest documents dealing with Kenwood are dated 1226 when William de Blemont (or Blemund) granted to the Priory of Holy Trinity, Aldgate, his lands in 'Kentistun' in the parish of St Pancras.[2] The following year the grant was confirmed by a royal charter issued by Henry III which refers to 'all his wood, with heath, and all appurtenances, as it is enclosed on all sides with ditches, in the Parish of St Pancras of Kentisseton, next to the park of the Lord Bishop of London, towards the south'.

William de Blemont was a member of the wealthy family of Blemont or Cornhill, of the City of London, who gave their name to Blemundsbury or Bloomsbury. The Priory of Holy Trinity, Aldgate, was an Augustinian Priory in the City of London; John Stow says that 'this Priorie in processe of time became a very fayre and large church, rich in lands and ornaments, and passed all the Priories in the citie of London, or shire of Middlesex'.

The documents do not refer to Kenwood by name but the reference to the Bishop of London's park (Hornsey Park) identifies the estate as covering the land we know as Kenwood and Parliament Hill. It was enclosed on all sides by ditches; the original Latin charter reads *'sicut undique fossatis includitur'*. Can we identify these medieval boundary ditches on the ground today?

We know that the western boundary of the estate was the manor boundary between Hampstead and Tottenhall which runs across the Heath today. A long stretch of this boundary follows an ancient ditch which starts where the footpath from Hampstead Ponds to the summit of Parliament Hill crosses another footpath leading from the railway bridge at Savernake Road to the western end of Ken Wood. The ditch follows this second footpath, keeping just to the left of it all the way; it lies between two banks, with a hedge of ancient oaks and hawthorns on the eastern bank. In the bed of the ditch parish boundary stones of Hampstead and St Pancras lie in pairs at irregular intervals.

After passing the western end of the Kenwood woodland, the ditch continues on the left of the footpath, accompanied by a wooden paling, which soon turns off sharply to the left. From here on the boundary is marked by a line of old oaks, two of which have parish boundary stones at their feet. This part of the ditch was evidently levelled by the Mansfields as part of the landscaping of Kenwood, but it existed as late as 1761 when it was mentioned in a survey of the manor of Tottenhall.

The ditch that we see today is clearly the western section of William de Blemont's boundary ditch, although it was certainly much deeper in his day. Continuity from 1226 to the present day is confirmed by a document of 1525 (see below) which refers to 'the great ditch' in exactly the same location.

Another very old hedge and ditch runs across Parliament Hill from east to west, just south of the summit of the hill; this was probably the southern boundary of the Blemont estate, since it is known to have been the boundary of Millfield Farm, the name given later to the southern part of the estate. Yet another hedge and ditch can be seen bordering the northern reaches of Millfield Lane; since this lane marked the eastern boundary of Kenwood, this is almost certainly the eastern part of the Blemont boundary ditch.

Most of the boundary ditches were doubtless made by one of William de Blemont's predecessors when he acquired the Kenwood estate from· St Paul's (which owned the manor of Tottenhall) at some date before 1226. But the western part, which was described as 'the great ditch' in 1525 and marks the ancient manor and parish boundaries, is probably older still and may well be Saxon.[3] A Saxon charter of Hampstead, dated AD 986, shows 'the hedge' as part of the eastern boundary of the manor.

Tudor Times

The Kenwood estate remained in the possession of Holy Trinity Priory for three hundred years, and the next document is dated 1525 when the estate was divided into two parts. The southern part, covering what we know as Parliament Hill, was a farm called Canewode Feildes or Millefeldes which was leased to Nicholas Gray, a yeoman of Highgate, while the northern part consisted of two large woods – Cane Wood and Gyll Holt.

In a grant dated 15 August 1525 the Priory appointed Nicholas Gray (presumably the same as above) as Woodward of these two northern woods. He was to oversee them and impound any animals that strayed into them; if he found anyone cutting or carrying away timber, he was to take them or report their names to the Prior; he was to scour the ditches and mend the hedges of the two woods, and also 'the great ditch between the upper end of the two fields called Mylfeld and Huntfeld and Hamsted Heth'. This ditch was on the boundary between the Kenwood estate and the Heath, and is clearly the same as de Blemont's boundary ditch.

Nicholas Gray was the last woodward appointed by the Priory. It was heavily in debt to the Crown and Henry VIII was able to exploit its difficulties. According to Stow he wanted to give the property of the Priory to Sir Thomas Audley, the speaker of the House of Commons, and persuaded the Prior to surrender it by promises of preferment. In 1532 the Priory was dissolved and its possessions vested in the Crown.

While the Priory itself was given to Sir Thomas Audley, the Kenwood estate was kept by the Crown. For some time Henry had cast longing eyes at the estate of Copt Hall in Epping Forest, 'to the whiche parke and mancyon house the Kynges highnes hathe a syngular pleasure and affeccion to repare and resorte for the great consolacion and comforde of his moste royall person'.[4] Copt Hall belonged to the great Abbey of Waltham, and Henry asked the Abbot to exchange it for Kenwood. The Abbot had little choice in the matter and Kenwood became the property of the Abbey, but in 1540 Waltham Abbey in turn was dissolved and Kenwood came back to the Crown.

At this point the two parts of the estate became separated and the southern end, the farm which covered Parliament Hill, was sold by the Crown in 1543. It is described as:

> all those lands, tenements, meadows, lesures, pastures, woods and underwoods lying . . . in the parish of St Pancras . . . now commonly called Millefeldes and Cane Woodfeldes, otherwise named Millefelde, Huntefeld, Fernefeld, Gutterfeld and Knyghtes Grove, lying together on the south side of Cane Wood and Gillishawte, lately belonging and appertaining to the late monastery of Waltham Holy Cross . . . now dissolved . . ., which lie and abut on Hachelane or Canewoodlane and the lands of John Palmer on the east, and on the said lands called Cane Woodde and Gillishawte on the north, and on Hampstede Heth on the west, and on the lands late Whitnalles on the south.[5]

This property became known as Millfield Farm and was later leased to the Hampstead Water Company.

In 1565 the Crown sold the wood which formed the northern part of the estate. In the Public Record Office is an early plan of this wood,[6] undated but probably made in the late sixteenth or early seventeenth century. It is endorsed 'A plott of the Wodes att Canewood' and has an accompanying description: 'This woode is knowen by the name of Cane Woode and conteyneth one hundred fower score and tenne acres, all wast and pathes deducted, and is devided into Tenne falls of diverse groathes with the valewe of evearie fall at Tenne yeares groath.' The plan shows the acreage and value of each 'fall' (the timber to be cut down in one season). Kenwood is often said to be a surviving fragment of the ancient forest of Middlesex, and this is true in the sense that it has probably been continuous woodland since prehistoric times. But it is certainly not virgin forest and was clearly managed as coppice woodland, and felled on a ten-year rotation, in the sixteenth century.

Although the plan in the Public Record Office is not exactly to scale, the outline of this large wood can easily be identified on a modern Ordnance Survey map (see map on p. 40). It stretched about half a mile from east to west and three-quarters of a mile from north to south, where it nearly reached Parliament Hill. The plan also names the pieces of land surrounding

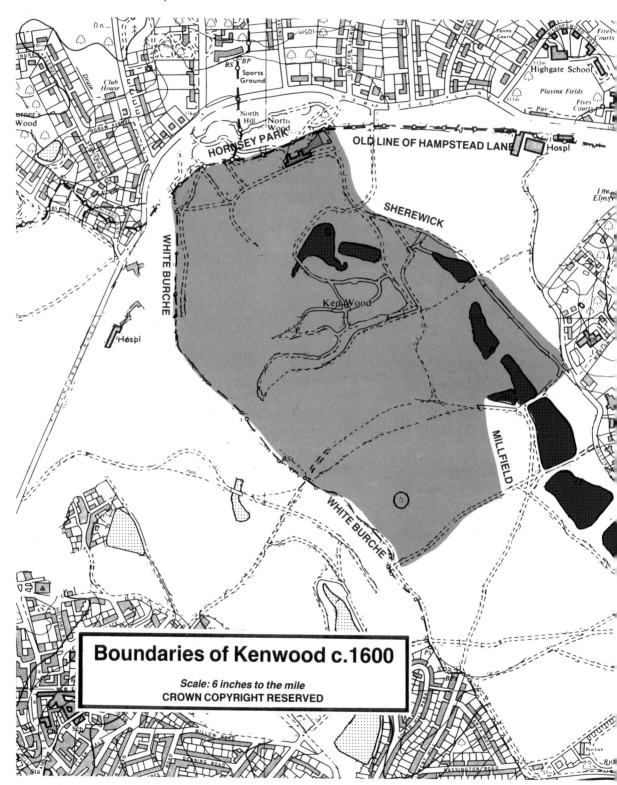

Boundaries of Kenwood c.1600

Scale: 6 inches to the mile
CROWN COPYRIGHT RESERVED

the wood. Beyond the western boundary (which is clearly the manor boundary with Hampstead) is marked 'White Burche', the wood recorded in the 1312 Valuation of Hampstead, which stretched along the boundary on the Hampstead side. This was probably felled and enclosed in the seventeenth century by the lord of the manor of Hampstead.

Beyond the northern boundary (the manor boundary with Hornsey) is marked 'Hornesey Park'. The Great Park of Hornsey or Haringey was the deer park of the medieval bishops of London, who were among the most powerful princes of the church. In the middle of this circular park, on Lodge Hill, stood the Bishop's Lodge, a country residence where the bishops often entertained royalty. This large hunting lodge, surrounded by an 800-foot moat, was in ruins in Tudor times and is shown as a 'decayde place' in John Norden's map of Middlesex in 1593. The remains of the moat can still be seen on Highgate golf course.

Beyond the eastern boundary of Kenwood are marked 'Sherewick' on the north-east, 'Sherewick Lane' on the east, and 'Millfeild' on the south-east. An old farm called Sherewick or Sherricks Farm lay on the north-east border of Kenwood; the earliest reference to it appears in a document of 1226 which refers to 'the wood of Sirewic'. Part of it now forms the north-east corner of the Heath, on the Highgate side of Kenwood. Sherewick Lane which led to the farm is now part of Millfield Lane; Millfeild was Millfield Farm, the southern part of the old Kenwood estate.

The Seventeenth Century

After the Crown sold Kenwood in 1565 it passed through several hands and was eventually bought by John Bill, the King's Printer, in 1616. It was he who built the first house on the estate, a substantial building rated at 24 hearths in the Hearth Tax assessment of 1665. He was succeeded by his son, also called John, who joined the royalist army during the Civil War and was heavily fined for his 'delinquency', being obliged to lease Kenwood in order to pay the fine. Despite this he became involved in a royalist insurrection soon afterwards and was fined a second time.

Shortly after the Restoration, in January 1661, Kenwood was involved in a strange incident when the Fifth Monarchy Men, a fanatical religious sect, staged a rising in London. Sir John Reresby, a Yorkshire squire who was a member of the court of Charles II, tells the story in his memoirs:

> In this month of Janu^r some discontented scismatics raised a small rebellion in London and were headed by one Venner their Capt, but were dispersed before they came to any considerable head by a party of ye Guards; the same night they went out of ye town & rallyed again in Canewood near High Gate, when a party of hors of ye Guards commanded by Sr Thom: Sands persued them. Being desirous to see a little Action, I took one of my Coachhorses & sett my man upon ye other, & joined Sr Thom: Sands (for I had noe saddle horses then in town). After seeking in ye wood till midnight by Moon shine, we came to a little hous wher ye people toald us they had been desireing victuals some time before, & that they could not be farr off. About one hour after we found some of them in ye thick part of ye wood, who discharged upon us with their muskits, but by reason of ye Moons setting gott from us, & marched into London again before break of day, when they were defeated by some of ye trainbands & ye hors Guards, their Capt^t taken prisner with about 20 more, & were all hanged drawn and quartered. They dyed

This Helmet was a Crown by Revelation
This Halbert was a Sceptor for the Nation.
So the Fifth-Monarchy anew is grac'd
King Venner next to John a Leyden plac'd.

21. Thomas Venner,
leader of the Fifth
Monarchy Men.

resolutely and unrepenting of their Crime. Some 20 of ye Rebels had been kild before in ye severall Skermishes, and as many of ye Kings men, one of wch was shott with a muskit bullet not far from me in Cane Wood.[7]

After the Restoration John Bill the younger continued to live at Kenwood with his wife, Lady Diana, a daughter of the Earl of Westmorland, until his death in 1680. His son, Charles Bill, sold the property in 1690 for £3,400; by this time a large part of the wood had been felled and converted into farmland.

The Jacobean house built by John Bill was replaced by a new red-brick house around the turn of the century. The house and farmland became separated and in 1712 the house was sold to the Duke of Argyll, who conveyed it three years later to his brother and brother-in-law, the Earls of Islay and Bute. They in turn sold it in 1720 to William Dale, an upholsterer of Covent Garden, who 'bought it out of the Bubbles'. When the South Sea Bubble burst the unlucky Dale was ruined and mortgaged Kenwood back to the Earl of Islay, who foreclosed in 1724 and recovered the estate.

In 1746 Kenwood passed to the third Earl of Bute, who was later to become the favourite and prime minister of George III. Bute's wife was the daughter of the famous Lady Mary Wortley Montagu, then living in Italy, who wrote to Lady Bute in 1749, 'I very well remember Caenwood House, and cannot wish you a more agreeable place. It would be a great pleasure to me to see my grandchildren run about in the gardens. I do not question Lord Bute's good taste in the improvements round it, or yours in the choice of furniture'.[8] Landscape gardening was one of Bute's hobbies but we do not know what improvements he carried out at Kenwood.

*22. William Murray,
first Earl of Mansfield
(J. S. Copley, 1783).*

The great Lord Mansfield

In 1754 Bute sold Kenwood for £4,000 to its most famous owner, William Murray, later Earl of Mansfield. Murray was the fourth son of an impoverished Scottish peer and had been packed off to Westminster School as a boy to get an education before making his career. He chose the legal profession and his outstanding ability, coupled with personal charm and great ambition, brought him immediate success at the Bar. At that time ambitious lawyers were expected to serve the government in the House of Commons if they wanted the highest judicial appointments, and Murray was serving as Attorney-General when he bought Kenwood. He was a very effective debater and one of the few men who could stand up to the elder Pitt in the House of Commons.

Two years later, when the Lord Chief Justice died, Murray claimed the office and held it for the next thirty-two years. He has been described in a recent biography as 'without question the greatest judge of the eighteenth century and one of the makers of English law'.[9] His most notable achievement was to bring order and principle into the commercial law of England, which had failed to keep pace with the country's growth into a great trading nation. He also introduced new legal procedures to reduce the endless delays and crippling costs of eighteenth-century litigation.

Mansfield was a man of wide culture who in his younger days, as Dr Johnson put it, 'drank champayne with the wits' and was a friend of Alexander Pope. When he wanted to remodel Kenwood House in 1764 he naturally turned to Robert Adam, a fellow Scot, who was then at the height

of his fame. Adam added a third storey to the house, built the magnificent library on the east side, and pulled together the whole south front with a pilastered stucco facade.

Lord Mansfield was responsible for landscaping the grounds, although the plan was Bute's according to a contemporary account.[10] Rocque's map of London in 1745 shows a formal garden and some small fishponds between the house and the wood. The garden was swept away and replaced by the 'natural' landscape of an eighteenth-century park in the style of 'Capability' Brown, with a grassy slope running down to two large sheets of water, while the wood provided the perfect backdrop. A delightful and little-known landscape painted by John Wootton in about 1760, *View from the Terrace at Kenwood* (Illustration 55), shows that most of the landscaping was carried out before that date.

The landscaping and natural beauty of the site gave the house a superb setting; Robert Adam describes the scene in his *Works in Architecture:*

> A great body of water covers the bottom, and serves to go round a large natural wood and tall trees rising one above another upon the sides of a hill. Over the vale, through which the water flows, there is a noble view let into the house and terrace, of the City of London, Greenwich Hospital, the River Thames, the ships passing up and down, with an extensive prospect, but clear and distinct, on both sides of the river. To the north-east, and west of the house and terrace, the mountainous villages of Highgate and Hampstead form delightful objects. The whole scene is amazingly gay, magnificent, beautiful and picturesque. The hill and dale are finely diversified; nor is it easy to imagine a situation more striking without, or more agreeably retired and peaceful within.

(Facing Page)
23. 'A View of Kenwood'
(G. Robertson, 1781)
before Humphry Repton's landscaping.

24. The north front of Kenwood, showing the walled courtyard and the road running close to the house (1788).

On the Hampstead side of Kenwood the famous advocate Thomas Erskine (later Lord Erskine) lived in a house which he called Evergreen Hill, next to the Spaniards Inn. An enthusiastic gardener, Erskine made a large garden on the other side of Spaniards Road, screened from the road by a holly hedge which can still be seen. The house and garden were connected by a tunnel under the road; this has now been filled in but one entrance can still be seen from the Heath.

The Mansfields' neighbour on the other side was Colonel Charles Fitzroy, younger brother of the Duke of Grafton, who later became Lord Southampton. He lived at Fitzroy Farm, a Palladian villa on the western slope of Highgate, surrounded by a park and a hundred-acre estate.

The Gordon Riots
For a week in June 1780, described by Dr Johnson as 'a time of terror', London was in the hands of the mob. The trouble started when the Protestant Association, led by Lord George Gordon, presented a petition to Parliament for the repeal of the Catholic Relief Act. The situation quickly got out of hand and in the next few days the London mob ran riot, pillaging and burning Catholic property, the prisons, and the houses of judges and magistrates.

Lord Mansfield, who was regarded as being pro-Catholic and a pillar of the establishment, was a special target. On the night of 6 June the mob attacked and burnt his town house in Bloomsbury Square and made a

Lord Southampton's Lodge, at Highgate, Middlesex?
Published 12 Sept.r 1792 by Rob.t Sayer & C.o Fleet Street London.

25. Fitzroy Farm, Lord Southampton's villa (1792).

bonfire of his furniture, pictures and valuable library; then they set out for his country house at Kenwood. According to the local historian Frederick Prickett,[11] the rioters stopped at the Spaniards Inn on their way to Kenwood. The landlord, Giles Thomas, showed considerable presence of mind, serving them liberally with liquor while sending a message for help. Another group of rioters gathered in the road outside Kenwood, which at that time ran close to the front of the house. John Hunter, Lord Mansfield's steward, supplied them with strong ale from the Kenwood cellars out of tubs placed by the roadside and by the time the troops arrived the rioters were in no condition to resist them.

Prickett's account, which has been repeated in every history of Hampstead and Highgate, is largely confirmed by two contemporary documents which are less well known. The first of these is a letter from Viscount Stormont, who was Mansfield's nephew and later succeeded him as the second Earl. At this time Stormont was Secretary of State for the Northern Department, and cabinet minister responsible for dealing with the riots. On the morning of 7 June (probably after receiving the appeal for help from Kenwood) he sent a message to Lord Amherst, the Commander-in-Chief of the Forces:

> St James, 7th June, 30m past 10 a.m.
> As there is great reason to believe that Lord Mansfield's house at Kenwood between Highgate and Hampstead is threatened with the same destruction that his house in town met with last night, I hope your Lordship will be so good as to order immediately a detachment of light horse for its protection. The servants there will point out the avenues that ought most to be secured.[12]

46

A detachment of light horse was sent to Kenwood, and the lieutenant in command later made his report:

> A party under my command, consisting of 18 privates and 2 non-commissioned officers of the 16th Lt. Dragoons and a N.C.O. and six of the Horse Grenadiers, march'd from the Horse Guards on Wednesday 7th inst. to Caen Wood, where I dispersed about 60 of the Rioters who had an intention of setting fire to Lord Mansfield's House. I returned from this duty at 8 o'clock in the evening of the same day.
>
> Wm. Bygrove
> Lieut. 16th Light Dragoons

Millfield Farm

Having acquired a fine house and park, Lord Mansfield set about rebuilding the Kenwood estate by purchasing the farmland to the south which had become separated from the house. Money was no problem since the office of Lord Chief Justice was the juiciest plum in the English legal profession, and Mansfield held it for thirty-two years, during which he amassed an enormous fortune. He had already made several additions to the estate when a major opportunity occurred in 1789. On 8 July the *Morning Herald* published an advertisement of a sale by auction:

> Highgate Ponds and Farm
> The Singularly Valuable and truly desirable Freehold and Tithe Free Estate, called Mill Field Farm . . . consisting of Three Spacious Lakes, called the Highgate Ponds which supply Kentish-Town and a great part of London with water, together with a Dwelling House, large Barn and other requisite Offices, an excellent Garden and Orchard, and sundry Inclosures of rich Meadow Land, containing together near Ninety Acres, lying within a Ring-fence.
>
> The beautifully elevated situation of this estate, happily rank it above all others round London, as the most charming spot where the Gentleman and the Builder may exercise their taste in the erection of Villas, many of which can be so delightfully placed as to command the richest home views of wood and water, and the distant views of the Metropolis, with the surrounding counties of Essex, Kent, Surrey and Berkshire.
>
> The whole of the Premises have been for more than a century in the occupation of the Hampstead Water Company on Lease, which expires at Michaelmas next, at a very low rent, but which is presumed to be little more than a quarter of the present value.

Millfield Farm, originally called Millefeldes, was the southern part of the former medieval estate which had been separated from the northern part in 1543. In the late seventeenth century the Hampstead Water Company had acquired the farm on a long lease and made three of the Highgate Ponds in the fields. The farmhouse at the foot of Millfield Lane, now called Millfield Cottage, is still standing although much altered.

The auctioneer's description of the property (which sounds curiously modern and familiar) was not exaggerated. The estate covered Parliament Hill and any houses built there would have had a magnificent view over London, although they might have been rather cold in winter. Fortunately Lord Mansfield had no intention of allowing an estate of villas, however desirable, to be built on the southern border of Kenwood; he purchased Millfield Farm himself and added it to the Kenwood estate. With this addition, the estate stretched from Hampstead Lane to just south of the

26. Long-horned cattle at Kenwood (J. C. Ibbetson, 1797).

summit of Parliament Hill, where the boundary is marked by an ancient hedge and ditch, covering some 232 acres in all (see map on p. 49).

The Second Earl

After his retirement Lord Mansfield spent all his time at Kenwood; he died there in 1793 and was succeeded by Lord Stormont, to whom he bequeathed the estate and his vast fortune. Stormont was 66 when he succeeded to the earldom and survived his uncle by less than four years. He had spent most of his life as a diplomat, serving as ambassador in Vienna and Paris, where he was visited by Lord Mansfield whom he presented to Louis XVI and Marie-Antoinette at Versailles. Although a man of ability and culture, he lacked his uncle's charm and was described by a contemporary as cold, haughty and ungracious.

After the death of his first wife Stormont married the 17-year-old Louisa Cathcart, a sister of the beautiful Mrs Graham of Balgowan painted by Gainsborough. Louisa's letters to her sister give some vivid glimpses of life at Kenwood. During her engagement she was taken to meet Lord Mansfield and wrote, 'Papa and I dined at Caen Wood (I am not sure if that is right spelt) and came home after nine o'clock without being robbed, which I think was a lucky escape.' A few months later Stormont and Louisa spent part of their honeymoon at Kenwood. By this time she had overcome her awe of

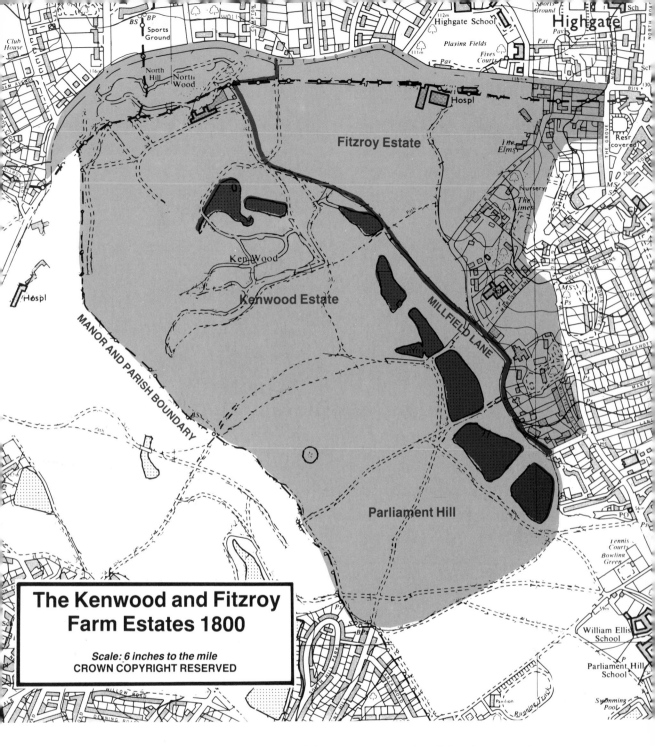

The Kenwood and Fitzroy
Farm Estates 1800

Scale: 6 inches to the mile
CROWN COPYRIGHT RESERVED

Lord Mansfield and told her sister, 'You did not see enough of Lord Mansfield to know how diverting he is, he says with the gravest face the most comical things imaginable. We are very well together.'[13]

When he succeeded his uncle in 1793 Stormont had already made his plans for improvements to Kenwood, and he earmarked £20,000 in his will for their completion. His architect, George Saunders, enlarged the house by adding two white-brick wings to the north front, containing the dining room

49

27. The second Earl of Mansfield.

and music room, and a new service wing, an attractive building of purple-brown brick on the east of the house. The old farm buildings were pulled down and a new octagonal farmhouse, with a layout designed by the agriculturalist William Marshall, was built near the western entrance from Hampstead Lane. A little further south, looking across the park, was a group of dairy buildings in the Swiss chalet style, now converted into staff cottages. On the other side of the house, near the eastern entrance from Hampstead Lane, new stables were built.

The second Earl was also responsible for pushing back the Hampstead-Highgate road which ran close to the house. By diverting it to the north the house was given complete seclusion, standing in its own park and approached by two winding carriage drives. The extension of the estate also provided more room for the new farm buildings and stables, while the wooded hill to the north of the house (then called Prospect Hill, now North Hill) made a fine addition to the park. The grounds added to Kenwood were part of Bishop's Wood, belonging to the Bishop of London.

The course of the old road, before it was diverted, can be traced through the grounds of Kenwood. Diverging from Hampstead Lane opposite the Spaniards Inn, it runs near the Dairy Cottage and the western car park. It then follows a line near the rhododendron walk and across the lawn north of the house before rejoining Hampstead Lane near the stables. The route can be traced by the ancient oaks which bordered the old road and also by some parish boundary stones, since the road followed the northern boundary of St Pancras parish.

The diversion of the road and replacement of the old farm buildings were part of a full-scale landscaping operation carried out by the second Earl. Plans of the estate made in 1793 and 1797 (in the Crace Collection at the British Museum) show that the whole of the grounds and gardens were

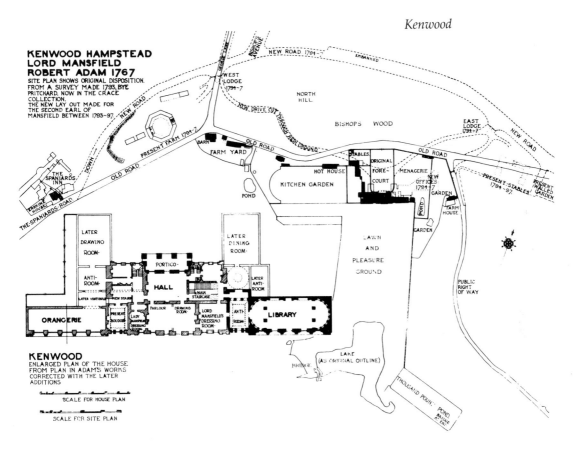

**KENWOOD HAMPSTEAD
LORD MANSFIELD
ROBERT ADAM 1767**
SITE PLAN SHOWS ORIGINAL DISPOSITION.
FROM A SURVEY MADE 1793, BYE
PRITCHARD. NOW IN THE CRACE
COLLECTION.
THE NEW LAY OUT MADE FOR
THE SECOND EARL OF
MANSFIELD BETWEEN 1793-97.

KENWOOD
ENLARGED PLAN OF THE HOUSE
FROM PLAN IN ADAM'S WORKS
CORRECTED WITH THE LATER
ADDITIONS

SCALE FOR HOUSE PLAN

SCALE FOR SITE PLAN

28. The landscaping of Kenwood between 1793 and 1797, showing the old and new layouts.

reshaped between these dates. The walled courtyard in front of the house was removed, and the two winding carriage drives were made from the house to the Hampstead-Highgate road. The land between the house and the lakes was opened out, hedges were cut down and winding walks made from both ends of the terrace down to the lakes. On the west of the house, the kitchen garden and outbuildings were replaced by lawns and flowerbeds.

This landscaping was largely the work of Humphry Repton, who was consulted by the second Earl in 1793, although others were also employed. Repton's writings indicate that he prepared one of his famous Red Books for Ken Wood showing the improvements he proposed to make, but it does not appear to have survived.[14]

[1] See map on p. 49.

[2] *Survey of London*, Vol. 17.

[3] *Hampstead and Highgate Express*, 10 March 1978. Article by David Sturdy.

[4] British Museum, *Harleian*. MS. 3739, ff. 427–9.

[5] Patent Rolls, 722. M. 27.

[6] MPF 293.

[7] British Museum, Add. MS 29440.

[8] *Survey of London*, Vol. 17.

[9] Edmund Heward: *Lord Mansfield* (1979).

[10] *Morning Herald*, 21 September 1781.

[11] Frederick Prickett: *Antiquities of Highgate* (1842).

[12] J. P. de Castro: *The Gordon Riots* (1926).

[13] E. Maxton Graham: *The Beautiful Mrs Graham* (1927).

[14] Humphry Repton: *Observations on the Theory and Practice of Landscape Gardening* (1803).

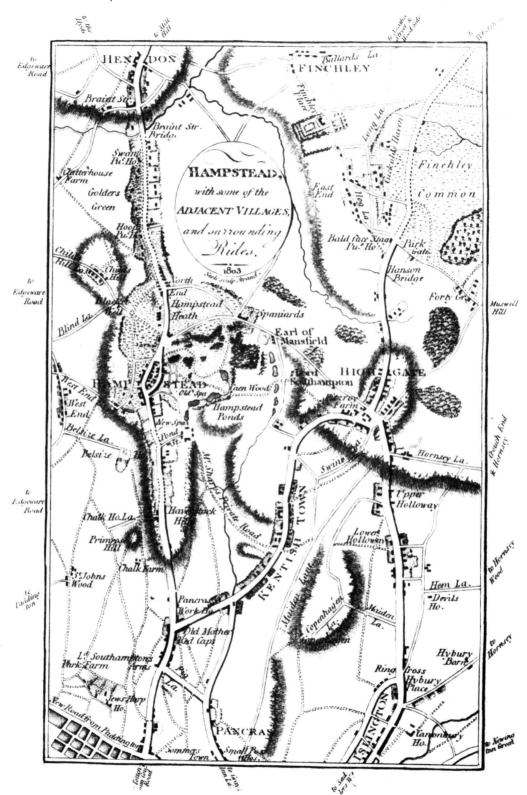

CHAPTER FOUR

Regency Times

Although Bonaparte's armies never reached the shores of England, the Napoleonic wars had their effect on Hampstead Heath. In 1798, when a French invasion was feared, volunteer corps were formed throughout the country. One of these was the Loyal Hampstead Association whose captain was Josiah Boydell, an engraver and print publisher who lived in West End; they had their exercise ground and shooting range on Hampstead Heath, in an area known as the Battery (between the Spaniards Road and the Vale of Health). In the summer of 1798 the Association, which was composed of 'Gentlemen and respectable Tradesmen of the vicinity', had a field day on the Heath; another gathering took place in October 1801, when there was a shooting contest followed by a dinner for 200 people in the Long Room in Well Walk, with loyal toasts and songs.[1]

During the brief peace of 1802–3 the Association was disbanded, but it reappeared as the Loyal Hampstead Volunteers, and the 700 members were presented with their colours at a ceremony in December 1803. Josiah Boydell, who had now been elected Colonel Commandant, made a rousing speech in which he compared them to Boadicea, Caractacus, Alfred the Great, Henry V and Queen Elizabeth.[2]

(Facing Page)
29. 'Hampstead with some of the Adjacent Villages' (1803).

Also part of the war effort was Telegraph Hill (just outside the Heath near the junction of West Heath Road and Platts Lane), which got its name at this time; it was previously called One Tree Hill. In 1798 a military telegraph station was erected on the hilltop, and ten years later the Admiralty built a line of stations from London to Great Yarmouth, which was in operation from 1808 to 1814. Telegraph Hill was one of the stations on this line, linking those at Chelsea Royal Hospital and Woodcock Hill, Elstree.

According to local legend James I used to make his base at Telegraph Hill when hunting on Hampstead Heath. Unfortunately this fine viewpoint was not part of the Heath and was not preserved when the latter was purchased for the public in 1871; the hill has now been covered with houses.

The Heath was also affected by the coming of peace. The winter of 1816 was a time of great distress and unemployment in England, and Hampstead tackled the problem by starting its own relief programme. However, this was sharply criticised in a newspaper report in December 1816:

> A subscription amounting to upwards of £500 has lately been raised at Hampstead, for the purpose of affording employment and relief to the labouring poor. This is truly laudable, and reflects great credit on the worthy inhabitants.
> It is to be lamented that their *taste* is not commensurate with their *benevolence*.

30. Spaniards Road, looking north towards the Spaniards (T. Hastings, 1823).

Will it be believed that at this moment there are near fourscore of these *parish pioneers* busily engaged with spades, shovels, pick-axes, wheelbarrows, and all the implements of rural destruction, in shaving, levelling, embanking and turfing Hampstead Heath? . . .

All those rude hillocks – sudden breaks – abrupt banks, and bold inequalities, with their varied tints of soil, of verdure, and of plants, which form the pre-ground of this extensive and picturesque view, the admiration of foreigners and the delightful study of our artists, are in danger of being reduced to a tame, formal, vapid smoothness, by the rash hands of *tasteless improvers* . . .

Nor is this all – for it is said that these well-meaning projectors, these new arbiters of taste, have it in contemplation to make – yes to make – an artificial piece of water on the north-west side of the Heath . . .

But really the matter becomes too serious for laughter. Hampstead Heath and Richmond Hill are, like *Shakespear* and *Newton*, the property of Europe, and must not be disfigured even for the purposes of charity.

Let then the intelligent Lady of the Manor, and the well-judging part of the inhabitants, immediately interfere to stop all further proceedings in a plan which will deform one of the most beautiful spots in the kingdom, and expose the neighbourhood to everlasting ridicule.[3]

Despite this vigorous protest the work went ahead. The 'artificial piece of water on the north-west side of the Heath' was probably the Leg of Mutton Pond which was made at about this time. A few years later, during a severe winter, the Sandy Road from North End to Telegraph Hill was raised and improved as another relief project; it was known as Hankins' Folly after Thomas Hankins, the parish overseer of poor relief.

Poets and Painters

Hampstead's golden age was the early nineteenth century, when the village and heath were discovered by the writers and painters of the Romantic movement. One of the first to arrive was Leigh Hunt, who came to live in the Vale of Health in 1815. With a deep feeling for Hampstead and the Heath, he captured the scene in one of his sonnets, which contains

references to the Vale of Health, Kenwood and Spaniards Road:

> A steeple issuing from a leafy rise,
> With farmy fields in front and sloping green,
> Dear Hampstead, is thy southern face serene,
> Silently smiling on approaching eyes,
> Within, thine ever-shifting looks surprise,
> Streets, hills and dells, trees overhead now seen,
> Now down below, with smoking roofs between, –
> A village, revelling in varieties.
> Then northward what a range – with heath and pond
> Nature's own ground, woods that let mansions through,
> And cottaged vales with pillowy fields beyond,
> And clump of darkening pines, and prospects blue,
> And that clear path through all, where daily meet
> Cool cheeks, and brilliant eyes, and morn-elastic feet.[4]

A man of many friends, Leigh Hunt was visited in the Vale by Byron, Hazlitt and Lamb among others. Keats sometimes spent the night there before he moved to Hampstead himself, and Shelley sailed paper boats on the pond to amuse Hunt's children.

On the other side of the Heath, Coleridge was living at The Grove in Highgate. His favourite walk was along Millfield Lane, then known for its nightingales; here he had his famous meeting with Keats, when Coleridge seems to have done most of the talking. In an amusing letter to his brother, Keats wrote that he 'walked with him at his alderman-after-dinner pace for near two miles . . . I heard his voice as he came towards me – I heard it as he moved away – I had heard it all the interval – if it may be called so'.[5] Coleridge also knew Kenwood well and wrote of the 'grand cathedral aisle of giant lime trees' on the terrace.

Hampstead Heath

Of the many artists who have lived in Hampstead, one of the first was the landscape painter John Linnell. He took a cottage in North End in 1822 and the following year rented part of Wyldes farmhouse; this was occupied by John Collins, a dairy farmer, and known as Collins' Farm. Linnell and his family lived at the farmhouse for five years and he painted many landscapes of the Heath. He was a close friend and admirer of William Blake, then in his sixties, who often visited Collins' Farm. Blake used to walk to the house across the Heath, where he was met and greeted by Linnell's children; in the evening, wrapped in a shawl by Mrs Linnell, he was escorted back to the road by a servant with a lantern. He was sometimes accompanied by the young Samuel Palmer who later married Linnell's daughter.

The greatest of the painters associated with the Heath was John Constable, who lived in Hampstead for many years. After renting summer cottages in 1819 and 1820 he took a longer lease on a house in Lower Terrace; the fresh air suited his wife and children and in 1827 he found a permanent home in Well Walk. The wild and unspoilt landscape of the Heath had a strong appeal for him, and his paintings give a good idea of its appearance

32. William Blake on Hampstead Heath (John Linnell).

in his day. There were very few trees. The open heath was covered with heather and gorse, and grazed by sheep, cattle and donkeys. The surface of the heath was scarred by sandpits, and the horses and carts of the sand-diggers can be seen in several pictures. Sand-digging had been carried on for centuries, and a 'gravell pit' near the beacon was mentioned by Gerard; the results can still be seen in the steep banks and hollows of the upper Heath.

33. 'Hampstead Heath: Branch Hill Pond' (John Constable, 1821). The West Heath from near Judges' Walk.

Another of Constable's subjects was the Firs Avenue, which the retired merchant John Turner had planted on the Heath close to his house at Heath End near the Spaniards. It was probably Constable's drawing of these pines (Illustration 34) which led William Blake to exclaim, 'Why, this is not drawing but inspiration!' (Constable replied rather drily, 'I never knew it before; I meant it for drawing.') This fine avenue was a well-known viewpoint, with an open outlook towards Harrow, and Coleridge used to come here to watch the sunset. Most of the great pines have now fallen but one or two still survive.

The Heath Keeper's Diary

In the 1830s the lord of the manor employed a Heath Keeper, an elderly man named John Stevenson, who kept a diary as a daily record of his work to be shown to Mr Lyddon, the steward. Stevenson was a 'character' and his

34. *'Fir Trees at Hampstead' (John Constable, 1820), showing the Firs Avenue.*

diary from 1834 to 1839, which has fortunately survived,[6] gives a vivid impression of the problems he had to contend with in carrying out his duties. It also allows us a rare glimpse of the common people of Hampstead, as distinct from the gentry.

One of Stevenson's duties was to stop unauthorised people from pasturing their animals on the Heath, and a cow-keeper from Fortune Green, appropriately called Mr Veale, caused him a lot of trouble:

> Aug 26, 1835 – I drove 59 cows of the Heath belonging to Mr Veale.
> Aug 28 – 60 cows.
> Aug 29 – 67 cows. Mr Veale occupies all fortin Green, no wright to Hampstead Heath.
> Oct 2 – Mr Veale is gon to live at the great Cow yard near the Ayre Arms Sant John's Wood.

At this time many of the villagers owned pigs, which roamed about the village and into the gardens of the gentry. A typical entry in the diary reads:

> Nov 2, 1835 – I am ashamed to see the Damige done by Hogs routing. I taken three home to Mrs Hicks. Damige great. Left word to send man to fill in Oales or I would put Law in force, she would Pay Dear for not bein Ruled and not ringing her hogs as it is the third time I have brought them home.

Stevenson was often asked to detain the wandering pigs in the village pound, which still stands between Whitestone Pond and the Vale of Health. On one occasion he impounded six hogs at the request of the vicar, Dr Samuel White, but the following night the owner broke the wall of the pound and rescued them. Stevenson appealed to the Steward in his diary, 'Sir, if you don't punish such a villion as this my labour will be in vain.'

35. The Village Pound (A. R. Quinton, 1911).

The Heath Keeper also had a lot of trouble with the village boys. On one occasion the 'climbing boys' employed by the village sweep cut furze on the Heath to make bonfires on Guy Fawkes' Day:

> Oct 29, 1834 – Mrs Herbert's sweep boys cutting furze for bonfires, went to see Mrs Herbert, going round North End, met boys with furze, boys ran away but two Young Gents of the swell mob stopt and struck at me with a fork. I rescued the fork and have got it at my house, they run away, I after them but they outrun me, fork marked L.R.
>
> Nov 5 – Ordered to look sharply after the boys Bonfires that no damage done to Heath.

On another occasion some boys set light to the furze bushes on the Heath itself, but they were caught by the police and taken before the magistrate:

> Oct 5, 1838 – I taken the boys befor Mr Plat with Hunt the Cunstable. Mr Plat promest to comit the next brought before him for triell but with my beging for murcey forgave them by paying the Cunstable Henry Hunt 2/6 each . . . If comited transportation 7 years, or two years Confinement and twice Whiped.

One of Stevenson's duties was to prevent the widespread theft of turf, sand and gravel from the Heath. This was usually done under cover of darkness and he often spent the night lying in wait for the offenders, taking another man with him for protection. On one occasion, without a companion, he was attacked:

> Nov 28, 1838 – Goin home between hours of 10 and 11 night I met a man name Wm. Green. He askd me to give him some Ale, I said no Sir, I dont know you, you have ad too mutch of what I have too Littell. He said you old Buger, Dont you know me, I owe you a grug now I will pay you. He upt with Both fistes, noct me down, falling with Boath Knees upon my Belley, I Cald out murder. I hollerd Police as Loud I Could oller, he Runaway.

Stevenson also kept an eye on the laundry-women who had been a feature of Hampstead for centuries. In the reign of Henry VIII, according to Park,[7] the clothes of the nobility, gentry and chief citizens used to be brought from London to be washed in the clean Hampstead water; the drying ground was the Heath, which in fine weather was white with linen spread over the broom and gorse bushes. In the nineteenth century there were still colonies of laundry-women in the Vale of Health, North End and Fortune Green; the washing was hung out on lines, where it was sometimes eaten by goats!

---

[1] Proceedings of Hampstead Antiquarian and Historical Society, 1899.
[2] Ibid.
[3] Newspaper cutting in the Local History Collection, Swiss Cottage Library (Ref H.712 5/A).
[4] Quoted in Hampstead Annual, 1897.
[5] Letters of John Keats, edited by Robert Gittings, 1970.
[6] Now in the Local History Collection, London Borough of Camden.
[7] J. J. Park, op. cit.

CHAPTER FIVE

The Heath under Attack

The year 1829 saw the opening of the long struggle to preserve Hampstead Heath and the adjoining lands from being covered with houses, and eventually to purchase them for the public.

Sir Thomas Spencer Wilson, the lord of the manor who made the grant to Mrs Lessingham, died in 1798. He was succeeded by his widow, Dame Jane Wilson, who was lady of the manor until 1818, and then by his son Sir Thomas Maryon Wilson, the seventh Baronet, who died in 1821; in his will the seventh Baronet divided his property between his sons.

His eldest son Thomas, the eighth Baronet, was to become the central figure in the long struggle over Hampstead Heath. On his father's death in 1821, this younger Sir Thomas became a wealthy man and a large landowner with estates in Kent, Sussex and Hampstead. He lived in style at Charlton House, a magnificent Jacobean mansion near Greenwich, and Searles, a country house near Uckfield in Sussex. As one of the leading landowners in Kent, he was later made Deputy Lieutenant of the county. Sir Thomas never married and his main interest in life, apart from managing the family estates, was the West Kent Militia of which he became Colonel.

As lord of the manor of Hampstead, Sir Thomas had manorial rights on the Heath. This was much smaller than it is today, comprising only the East, West and Sandy Heaths (see map on p. 105); Kenwood, Parliament Hill, Golders Hill Park and the Heath Extension were still private property.

In addition to his rights on the Heath, Sir Thomas was the largest landowner in Hampstead. His main estate of 356 acres, in what is now the Finchley Road district, was the old demesne land which had belonged to the lord of the manor since medieval times; still farmland in 1829, it was known as the Manor Farm (Illustration 37). Sir Thomas also owned 60 acres of private farmland adjoining the East Heath – the land once covered by White Burche Wood. These fields are now part of the Heath, but in 1829 they separated the East Heath from Kenwood and Parliament Hill. Sir Thomas Wilson's attempts to build on this land (later known as the East Park estate) were at the centre of the struggle for the Heath.

Under his father's will, however, the estates were entailed, and Sir Thomas was only tenant-for-life, with power to grant short agricultural leases for not more than 21 years. In 1821, shortly before his death, his father made two codicils to his will, giving his son power to grant 70-year building leases on his properties at Woolwich and Charlton in Kent, but they did not affect Hampstead, where he could neither sell the property nor grant

36. Sir Thomas Maryon Wilson.

building leases. The elder Sir Thomas therefore made a deliberate distinction between the Woolwich and Charlton property and the Hampstead property, on which he evidently did not want his son to build; this was to be of vital importance in saving Hampstead Heath.

The First Round, 1829–30

After the death of the elder Sir Thomas in 1821 the situation changed, since his son did not share his anxiety to protect Hampstead from development. In 1826 Parliament approved the building of a new turnpike road, the Finchley Road, which was to run straight through Manor Farm, the main Maryon Wilson estate in Hampstead. The new road increased the value of the estate, which became potential building land, and Sir Thomas was not slow to realise the truth of a rhyme published some years later:

> The richest crop for any field
> Is a crop of bricks for it to yield.
> The richest crop that it can grow
> Is a crop of houses in a row.

Between Sir Thomas and this rich harvest stood his father's will, and in 1829 he decided to seek powers to alter the will and grant building leases in Hampstead. As the law stood at the time, there were two ways in which this

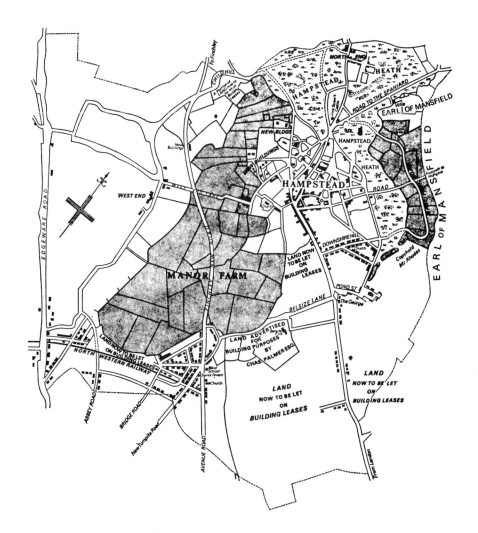

37. Hampstead in 1853, showing the two Maryon Wilson estates (shaded).

could be done. First, the tenant-for-life could wait until his own son and heir reached the age of 21 and then agree with him to alter the family settlement; but Sir Thomas never married, so this course was not open to him. The alternative was to obtain a private Act of Parliament amending the settlement, and he promoted a series of Estate Bills to this end.

Private Estate Bills were introduced in the House of Lords, and in 1829 Sir Thomas submitted one seeking power to grant 99-year building leases on his Hampstead property – that is, the large Finchley Road estate and the smaller estate adjoining the Heath. In his petition in support of the Bill he said that his father's failure to give him such powers was simply an oversight.

In saying this Sir Thomas was perjuring himself. We know this because of a statement that he made in 1824 when he was opposing the proposal to build the new Finchley Road turnpike across his estate. In the statement of his case he referred to the two codicils made by his father in 1821, to allow building leases at Charlton and Woolwich, and went on to say 'but upon his being asked if he would do the like as to the Hampstead Property, he said no; and expressed his sentiments for leaving that as it was.'[1] This important admission makes it quite clear that the father's failure to give his son building powers in Hampstead was not an oversight but a deliberate intention. Fortunately for Sir Thomas, his opponents in the Heath dispute were unaware of this statement; if they had known of it, it is unlikely that any of his Estate Bills would even have got a hearing, since Parliament would not have been prepared to override his father's clear intention.

The main purpose of his 1829 Bill was to give Sir Thomas power to grant building leases on the two Hampstead estates, but he or his advisors unwisely tacked on to it two additional clauses: the 'copyhold clause' and the 'Heath clause'. The first of these dealt with a minor point but the second had much wider implications since it empowered the lord of the manor to grant building leases on any parcels of land that he enclosed *from the Heath itself*. It is not clear whether Sir Thomas had any immediate intention of building on the Heath, or whether the clause was only added in case he wanted to do so in the future, but in either case it was a direct threat to the Heath.

The Hampstead copyholders had not been given notice of the Bill and were unaware of it until one of the peers (possibly Lord Mansfield) drew attention to it in a letter to a Hampstead friend. A notice was then read out after service in the parish church, calling a meeting of copyholders and inhabitants, and a petition against the Bill was drawn up for presentation to the House of Lords. At this stage the copyholders were concerned only about the copyhold clause, which, they were advised, would interfere with their right to build on their own copyholds. This point was met by an amendment protecting their rights, after which the Bill passed the House of Lords and went to the Commons. But some of the smaller copyholders were more concerned about the 'Heath clause'; they took over the Copyholders' Committee and organised a second petition to the Commons.

This was presented to the House by Robert Gordon, the member for Cricklade, and there was a short debate. Gordon was opposed by Sir Charles Burrell, a Sussex landowner like Sir Thomas Wilson, who 'thought that the Lord of the Manor of Hampstead ought not to be precluded from improving his property with the consent of the copyholders, because the tradesmen of the Metropolis chose to make it a place of recreation for themselves, their wives, children and friends'. This brief debate alerted the press and public, and on 16 June the *Morning Herald* launched an attack on the Bill in a leading article:

> We have more than once noticed the objectionable Bill now in progress through the Commons, to enable the Lord of the Manor of Hampstead to enclose the Heath, and are happy to see it is vigorously opposed. Sir Chas. Burrell, who can retire to his estate in Sussex for recreation, may think it unnecessary that the Heath should be preserved as 'a place of recreation for the tradesmen of the metropolis, their wives, children and friends' but if he were confined to a sedentary trade for six days out of the seven, in sooty London, he would probably argue differently. The comforts of the lower classes are too much neglected by the Aristocracy of the country, and we do hope that this attempt to deprive 'tradesmen' of the pleasures of fresh air, will be defeated.

A leader in *The Sun* was more outspoken:

A Bill is now in progress through the House of Commons, the avowed object of which is to enable the Lord of the Manor to enclose Hampstead Heath. We cannot too strongly protest against this outrageous Act, which violates every principle of good taste, feeling, and policy.

Hampstead Heath has long been looked on by the majority of respectable London tradesmen and their families as a place of chosen resort, whenever their leisure enables them to turn their backs on the close, pent-up, and smoky streets of the metropolis. In point of air, it is well-known and much esteemed for its salubrious properties, and hence during the summer months, hundreds of families resort to it on the same principle that they would resort (could they afford it) to Cheltenham or some such fashionable watering-place. The present Bill, however, if permitted to pass, will go far to reduce it to the level of Brentford, Isleworth, and such like smoke-invested towns; and by depriving it nearly, if not wholly, of its salubrious character, will materially interfere with the interests of its inhabitants. And pray at whose request is this delightful Heath to be enclosed? At the prayer, forsooth, of the Lord of the Manor, to whose individual interests hundreds of respectable tradesmen are, it seems, to be offered up as victims. We say nothing of the disinterested spirit that has dictated this request; it sufficiently speaks for itself, but we may at least be permitted to comment upon the good taste that recommends the choking up and suffocating the prettiest, the healthiest, the most picturesque spot for miles about London, with a coarse, unsightly mass of bricks and mortar, which, agreeably to the principles of modern architecture, if built up into something like houses this year, will most assuredly tumble down the next.

The public was now up in arms, and when the Bill was debated in the Commons there was no doubt about the mood of the House. In moving the Bill's rejection, Robert Gordon based his case on grounds of public policy:

Even if all the copyholders had consented to the measure, he should object to it on the behalf of the public. It was not the fashion of the day to think much about the amusements or comforts of the poorer classes of society; but he nevertheless contended, that the House was bound not to do anything that might tend to abridge those comforts or amusements. Besides, it was not merely the poorer classes of society that were interested in this question; for he would venture to say, that there was not a gentleman who resided in the vicinity of Hampstead that did not derive a benefit, either for himself or for his family, from having access to the heath. If the lord of the manor already possessed the right of building there, let him have it; but he must protest against any further facilities being afforded for the prosecution of so undesirable an object.[2]

Gordon was supported by several other members and the only voice raised in support of the Bill was that of Spencer Perceval, a cousin of Sir Thomas Wilson, who had been briefed to attend by Sir Thomas' solicitor. In view of the strong opposition he was forced to withdraw the Bill without a division.

The strength of public feeling was reflected in George Cruikshank's well-known print *London Going Out of Town* (Illustration 38), a comment on the expansion of London in general and Sir Thomas Wilson's Bill in particular. The meadows around London with their trees, hayricks and cattle are being attacked by an army of builders' tools and chimneypots, supported by a cannonade of bricks from a brick kiln; behind the advancing army spring up rows of jerry-built houses marked 'New Street'. In one corner of the picture a signpost points to Hampstead, where one tree is saying to another, 'Our fences I fear will be found to be no defence against these Barbarians who threaten to enclose & destroy us in all "manor" of

Within the illustration, handwritten text includes signs and captions:

"This Ground to be Let on Building Lease. Inquire of Mr Goth Brick maker Bricklayers Arms Brick Lane Brixton"

"NEW STREET"

"Rubbish may be shot here"

"Hey day! come along my little bricks, we must go farther afield, for we are losing ground here"

"Our fences I fear will be found to be no defence, against these Brick-a-nians who threaten to enclose & destroy us in all 'manor of ways'. Detachments are on the R—"

"Confound these Brick kilns. They'll be the death of us all"

"O! I'm Mortarly wounded!!"

38. London going out of town (George Cruikshank, 1829).

(Facing Page)
39. London from Hampstead Heath (F. Nash, 1830).

40. The West Heath (C. Marshall, 1832).

ways. Detachments are on the Road already.'

Sir Thomas renewed his attack in 1830, when he presented a new Bill again seeking power to grant building leases on his two Hampstead estates, but this time omitting the 'Heath clause'. If the Bill had been introduced in this form the previous year it would undoubtedly have been passed, but the 1829 campaign had served to alert both the Hampstead copyholders and public opinion.

At this time the East Heath was only a narrow strip of land running from the Hampstead Ponds to the Spaniards Road (Illustration 37). On one side of it was the built-up area of Hampstead Village, and on the other lay the 60-acre estate of Sir Thomas Wilson, later known as the East Park Estate. If Sir Thomas had been allowed to build on this estate, the East Heath would have been almost entirely surrounded by houses, and cut up by two or three access roads needed to connect the estate with the rest of Hampstead.

Because of this the Hampstead copyholders decided to oppose the new Bill. Their strongest argument was the failure of Sir Thomas Wilson's father to give his son power to grant building leases on the two Hampstead estates, although giving him that freedom at Charlton and Woolwich. The new Bill was therefore an attempt to override his father's deliberate intention. This argument, which found the weakest point in Sir Thomas' case, was to dog him for the next forty years. It was put forward by the third Earl of Mansfield when the Bill was debated in House of Lords and strongly supported by the Lord Chief Justice, Lord Tenterden; when the House divided the Bill was defeated by 23 votes to 7.

The Second Round, 1843–4

After his defeats in 1829 and 1830 Sir Thomas took no further action for some years, probably because the building recession of the 1830s gave him no immediate incentive to develop his property, but in 1843 he came forward with a new Bill, again seeking power to grant building leases on his two Hampstead estates. Once again the argument centred round the 60 acres of private farmland between East Heath and Parliament Hill. Sir Thomas argued that this was Maryon Wilson property and he was entitled to build on it if he wished, but his opponents replied that this would destroy the beauty of the Heath, as his father had recognised by protecting it in his will.

On 15 May a public meeting was held in Hampstead with Samuel Hoare (the younger) in the chair. In the next thirty years the Hoare family were to play a leading part in defending the Heath. Samuel Hoare the elder, a Quaker banker and philanthropist, had come to live in Hampstead in 1790. His son, also called Samuel, followed the family tradition of banking and philanthropy, and his grandson, John Gurney Hoare, was to be known as the man who saved the Heath.

The meeting was addressed by the Rev. Allatson Burgh, after whom Burgh House is named, and Thomas Toller, the secretary of the copyholders' committee. It then approved a petition against Sir Thomas' Bill and appointed a committee to 'take all measures necessary for a most determined opposition'. There was strong support from the national press, and the *Morning Herald* attacked the Bill in an editorial:

> At a time when every exertion is being made by Government to throw open the hitherto restricted places of healthful enjoyment, to embellish on the one hand and to create on the other; when the public mind has become sensitively alive to the necessity of retaining its right to the little that is left of the open spaces which once surrounded London, an attempt is being made by certain interested parties to deprive myriads of almost the only enjoyment within their reach, and to shut out the free air of Heaven from the toiling mechanic and the feeble invalid, by covering Hampstead-heath with bricks and mortar, and this under the guise of 'improvement', a cant word which, being truly interpreted, signifies simply personal profit.[3]

The Pictorial Times joined in with a front-page article on 'The March of Bricks and Mortar':

> This is the third time that an attempt has been made to legalise the robbery of the public by depriving them of the solace of Hampstead Heath. If any poor wretch, lurking thereabout, were to pick a man's pocket of a cotton handkerchief, why there would be the House of Correction or the Model Prison for him; but steal, by Act of Parliament, acres and acres, and the stolen goods return a handsome profit to the evil-doer.
>
> The people of Hampstead have been on the alert – have met, and caused a wary watch to be set in Parliament on the movements of Sir Thomas Wilson. But it is not the people of Hampstead so much as the people of Fleet Street and the Strand – nay, so much as the people of the courts and alleys of the metropolis, who are interested, we may say vitally interested, in the question. Cover Hampstead Heath with bricks and mortar, the people living there may yet escape to neighbouring fields; but how much farther off does it place a spot of health and recreation for the Londoner?[4]

This was stirring stuff although it was of course unfair to Sir Thomas, who was not trying to build on the Heath itself but on the adjoining fields; however, he himself was partly to blame for the confusion. In his 1829 Bill he certainly had in mind enclosing and building on parts of the Heath, and he repeatedly claimed that he had the right to do this. The outcry in 1829 led to all his later Bills being regarded as Enclosure Bills despite his indignant denials. Indeed they were Enclosure Bills in one sense, as the Heath defenders pointed out, since his building plans would have meant enclosing the East Heath with houses. In any case, Sir Thomas could hardly complain of misrepresentation by the press since he himself had already committed the much more serious offence of perjury.

The dispute came to a head when the petition against the Bill, signed by '500 most respectable persons', including most of the leading residents of Hampstead, was presented to the House of Lords by Lord Brougham, the radical former Lord Chancellor. In the face of this opposition Sir Thomas had to accept defeat, and he withdrew the Bill on the day appointed for its second reading in the Lords.

Sir Thomas was an obstinate man, however, and he tried again the following year. This time he sought power to sell the whole of his Hampstead property, lock, stock and barrel; by so doing he would have achieved his object since he could expect to get a full building price for the land. But from the public's point of view the Bill was open to the same objection as the earlier ones since the purchaser, having paid a building price for the land, would clearly waste no time in building on it and, furthermore, would not be restricted by the provisions of the will.

41. Downshire Hill from the Lower Heath (G. S. Shepherd, 1833).

In the debate in the House of Lords the Bill was supported by two large landowners, the Earl of Egmont (a cousin of Sir Thomas) and the Earl of Wicklow, who argued that thirty similar Bills had been approved by the House in the previous ten years. As to the public interest, the Earl of Wicklow said that 'he did not at all agree with the argument that they should deprive one individual of privileges enjoyed by others, because by adopting a different course they might somewhat trench upon some supposed advantages to be derived by the public'. But the Lord Chief Justice, quoting the elder Sir Thomas' will, said it would be wrong to contravene his deliberate intention merely because it was inconvenient for his son, and the Bill was rejected. Twist and turn as he might Sir Thomas could not escape from his father's will.

The East Park Estate

While he had no power to grant building leases on his Hampstead estates, Sir Thomas was free to build houses himself if he could find the money. Having lost four Estate Bills, his next plan was to develop the meadowland adjoining the East Heath out of his own pocket. He made this clear in a letter to Henry Sharpe, a well-known Hampstead resident with whom he was on friendly terms:

> I am about to carry out all my projects for the improvement of my property to the full without the aid of Parliament which aid could have only made the difference of my doing that with the monies of others which I shall now do with my own, and so put *both* Landlords and Builders *profits* into my Pocket, and that which I shall do shall be a standing answer to the lies and falsehoods of Mansfield, Hoare, Toller and Co.

Sir Thomas explained that he intended to build the houses with his own bricks: 'I have made a Batch of Bricks from Hampstead Clay. I sent into Sussex for some Brickmakers, who are the best, and built a Kiln here [i.e. at Charlton] to try the experiment which *answers*.'[5]

He started operations in October 1844 – without informing anyone of his intentions. A report in *The Times* suggested that he was going to build a cemetery:

> The inhabitants of Hampstead . . . have been in much consternation during the past week, upwards of 80 workmen having been employed in levelling the fences between the various fields belonging to Sir Thomas between the Vale of Health and Highgate . . . Sir Thomas' property immediately adjoins Caen-wood, the grounds of which will be commanded by the intended cemetery.[6]

Sir Thomas was in fact laying out the ground for building. He planned to convert the meadows adjoining the Heath into a park with twenty-eight villas, to be christened the East Park (not to be confused with the East Heath). His architects submitted their plan in November (Illustration 42). It shows a road running through the middle of the estate, from the Vale of Health to Hampstead Ponds, with a lodge at each entrance to the park. Each villa is set in two acres of ornamental grounds and separated from its neighbours by a belt of trees. A large rectangular area on each side of the

(Facing Page)
42. Sir Thomas Wilson's plan for villas on the East Park estate (1844).

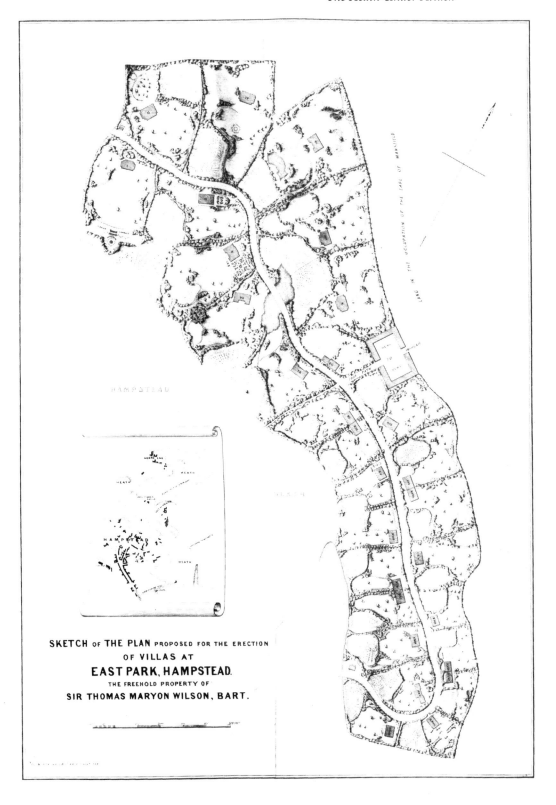

SKETCH of **THE PLAN** PROPOSED FOR THE ERECTION
OF VILLAS AT
EAST PARK, HAMPSTEAD.
THE FREEHOLD PROPERTY OF
SIR THOMAS MARYON WILSON, BART.

path to Highgate is laid out as mews. Sir Thomas made the road through the estate which can still be seen on the Heath today. So can the wall that marked the park boundary near the Vale of Health, and the brick hut with a conical roof (possibly for the gatekeeper) which was built nearby. Near the road the foundations of a house were begun, and a few courses of bricks laid, while a nursery of young trees and shrubs was planted to stock the gardens of the villas.

As to the adjoining East Heath, Sir Thomas intended to convert it into an ornamental park 'as a place of recreation for my own houses' (as he later told the Select Committee of 1865). To make it more park-like he planted hundreds of willows, with some firs and Turkey oaks, and at Charlton he grew 'a very large collection of Cedar trees and curious oak trees' to be planted later. Charles Dickens, who knew the Heath well and often walked over it, objected strongly to the newly planted trees; some years later, in 1857, he asked in his paper *Household Words*:

> Who planted them? Had he any business to do so? They are an eyesore. Where will they end? Did not some one say that somebody – we forget, and do not care who – tried to enclose Hampstead Heath? If he does so, may his heirs find a quick road to their inheritance! . . . It must have been . . . some half-fledged baronet, the second of the family, who having a half title to his own property, fancied that no title at all might suffice for appropriating that of the public. Whoever he was, may his dreams be redolent of Smithfield, may nightmare tread with donkey hoofs on his chest, and may visions of angry laundresses scald his brain with weak tea!

Sir Thomas' most ambitious project was to build a brick viaduct to carry his road across a swampy valley in the middle of the estate. The laying of the first stone was stage-managed to win support for his building plans, and a full report of the ceremony appeared in *The Times*:

> The work being situate in a hollow the ground around it forms a natural amphitheatre, and the event being regarded altogether as a public one by the worthy inhabitants of Hampstead, a considerable number of persons had assembled·to witness the ceremony. The hour fixed was 2 o'clock for 3; and shortly before the latter hour a band of musicians marched to the ground and began to amuse the assembled company by a variety of lively airs, not forgetting the never tiring polka. They were followed by a party of amateur 'artillery', who mounted their pieces on the heights, ready to announce the auspicious event by a discharge of cannon. In a few minutes Sir Thomas Maryon Wilson and a numerous party of relatives and friends arrived; among them was his sister, Mrs Drummond, a charming lady, who had been selected to perform the ceremony of laying the first stone. Mrs Drummond was conducted to the platform by Mr Gwilt, the architect; and, all being in readiness, she spread the mortar with a silver trowel made for the occasion, in a most business-like manner, and, the level having been applied, struck the stone three times, with a masonic precision which called forth a hearty burst of cheers, and the block was let down to its resting-place amid a discharge of cannon and continued cheering, the band meanwhile playing the national anthem. As soon as the ceremony was over, the workmen partook of a dinner provided for them, at the expense of Sir Thomas Wilson, in a marquee on the Parliament hill, and Sir Thomas also entertained a party of friends at his own house.[7]

The swampy valley was drained to form an ornamental pond, the Viaduct Pond. However, owing to the nature of the soil and the presence of springs, the excavations required for the viaduct (known subsequently as Wilson's Folly) repeatedly collapsed; in all, the work took three years to complete.

41586. Hampstead, Viaduct &c .F.F.&Cº

In digging the viaduct's foundations the workmen found various strange objects in the swamp which throw a curious light on the history of the area. They included several stone and bronze axes; a number of fine large agates; part of a large antler of a deer; part of a wild boar's tusk; some old keys, rings and coins; a fleam for bleeding cattle; a fish's tooth – apparently a shark's; and a human skull with two holes knocked into it.[8]

This was as far as Sir Thomas went in developing the East Park estate out of his own pocket. He must have realised that the scheme was beyond his resources, and he returned to his earlier plan to seek power to grant building leases from Parliament.

43. The Viaduct built by Sir Thomas Wilson.

Mr Cockerell's Plan

In 1853 two important developments took place. Sir Thomas Wilson introduced a new Estate Bill which will be described later. At the same time, an ambitious and imaginative scheme was prepared for the government to purchase the Heath, with certain adjoining lands, and create what was described as Hampstead New Park. This plan seems to have been a response to Sir Thomas' threat, in his latest Estate Bill, to build on the East Park and Telegraph Hill. It was drawn up by the distinguished architect C. R. Cockerell, designer of the Ashmolean Museum at Oxford, who lived at North End in Hampstead, but the initiative may have come from the Heath defenders led by Gurney Hoare.

PUBLIC PARK, HAMPSTEAD-HEATH.

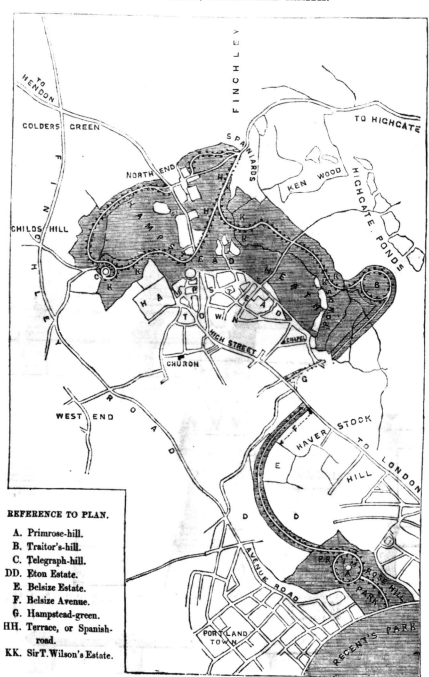

REFERENCE TO PLAN.

A. Primrose-hill.
B. Traitor's-hill.
C. Telegraph-hill.
DD. Eton Estate.
E. Belsize Estate.
F. Belsize Avenue.
G. Hampstead-green.
HH. Terrace, or Spanish-
     road.
KK. Sir T. Wilson's Estate.

44. C. R. Cockerell's plan for Hampstead New Park (1853).

The history of this scheme is an interesting and little-known episode in the story of the Heath. A plan published in *The Builder* (Illustration 44) shows the Heath, the East Park, Parliament Hill and Telegraph Hill combined to form the new park. Its layout suggests that Cockerell based his plan on Nash's Regent's Park. It was also proposed to purchase a strip of land in Belsize Park, 300 feet in width, through which a carriage drive or boulevard would run; this would link the new park with Primrose Hill and also run round the borders of the park itself. The course of the carriage drive, after leaving Belsize Park, was described as follows:

> The course thence is by Hampstead-green passing over another commanding eminence known as Traitor's Hill [Parliament Hill] from which an admirable view of London and surrounding scenery presents itself, through land now desired to be built over and which, if so appropriated, would for ever deface the beautiful locality. From this ground the road mounts to the Royal-terrace across the Heath [Spaniards Road] appreciated alike by the monarch and the mechanic, and continues to the well-known firs [the Firs Avenue] from whence is enjoyed a lovely view of Harrow and the western country, unsurpassed by the imaginings of Claude and Turner. In the enjoyment of this beautiful scenery we descend the Heath to a hamlet designated North-end, and proceed around its western verge to a third commanding height called Telegraph-hill, which, as its name implies, is a land-mark through the country, and again displays to us a new and enchanting panorama. Here we arrive at a further portion of the ground desired to be appropriated for building, but which this project would secure as a necessary adjunct to the enjoyment of the Heath; passing through this land, the road would return to the upper terrace.[9]

The Hampstead Vestry called a public meeting on 22 June 1853 to discuss this plan, and a resolution was passed urging the government to make the purchase. The meeting also approved a Memorial to the Commissioners of Woods and Forests, setting out in detail the land that would have to be bought and its cost, and appointed a 30-strong committee to present the plan. This deputation, probably led by Gurney Hoare, obtained an interview with the prime minister; the outcome was described by Philip Le Breton, one of the leading Heath defenders, in his evidence to the Select Committee of 1865:

> A deputation of the inhabitants of Hampstead, accompanied by others, I believe also by some of the artists of London, who took a great interest in the preservation of the Heath, went to Lord Aberdeen with this plan, to which he was extremely favourable, and we endeavoured to obtain a grant of money for it; but he stated that the whole expense could not be borne by Government without some local contribution. There was then no Metropolitan Board of Works and no means of obtaining any contribution from the metropolis generally, and so the plan fell through.

The stumbling-block was that at this time there was no local authority for London which could raise money for the benefit of Londoners. As things turned out it was perhaps fortunate that the scheme did fall through, since it would have turned Hampstead Heath into another version of Regent's Park with a scenic carriage drive for the gentry. Nevertheless, the Cockerell plan was a major step forward, setting out for the first time a detailed and imaginative scheme for the Heath to be purchased and preserved for the public; it also recognised that the Heath alone was not enough, and the adjoining lands such as East Park and Parliament Hill must be added. It was

*45. The Sandy Road
from the Spaniards to
North End (G. Childs,
c.1840).*

*46. John Gurney Hoare
(G. Richmond, 1855).*

to take many years and many battles before Cockerell's vision was realised.

The Third Round, 1853–4

While the Heath defenders were pressing the government to adopt the Cockerell plan, they were also fighting off Sir Thomas Wilson's fifth Estate Bill, which he introduced early in 1853. As usual he gave no notice of his plans to the people of Hampstead, but after the Bill was published his solicitor, William Loaden, called a public meeting on 1 June in the Hampstead Assembly Rooms. It was very crowded and Loaden's opening statement was followed by 'some conversation of angry character'. Gurney Hoare made a strong attack on Sir Thomas and his Bill, arguing that building powers had been deliberately withheld by Sir Thomas' father, and that he should consult the people of Hampstead if he wanted to build on the East Park. He then moved a resolution that 'this meeting consider that the passing of this bill will be highly detrimental to the interests of the public in general, as well as the inhabitants of this place'.[10]

Gurney Hoare is generally regarded as the man who saved the Heath. This is, of course, an over-simplification, since campaigns were led by different men at different times, but Gurney Hoare is entitled to the lion's share of the credit since he took the lead in the 1850s and 1860s when the hardest battles were fought. John Gurney Hoare was the second son of Samuel Hoare the younger, but his elder brother died young. He went to Trinity College, Cambridge, and in due course became senior partner in the family bank, Barnett Hoare and Co of Lombard Street, where he maintained the family eminence in the City. He and his wife Caroline lived at The Hill, a large Georgian house off North End Way on the site now occupied by Inverforth House. He was chairman of the bench of magistrates, a member of the Vestry, and was generally regarded as the squire of Hampstead. A man of genuine warmth and kindness, Hoare was a popular figure in Hampstead, involved in many aspects of community life.

Under his leadership the Heath defenders mustered their forces once again after the meeting on 1 June. This time they found a valuable ally in *Punch*, then a radical paper, which contributed a song entitled 'The Witches on Hampstead Heath' to be sung by 'Sir Th-m-s W-ls-n':

> I'll build and plant on Hampstead Heath,
> To gain more land by Daddy's death;
> Four times I've tried this trick to do,
> Having his wishes not in view;
> And so I'll break my Father's Will,
> By smuggling through the Lords a Bill,
> While some new law 'bout trade or crime
> Absorbs the Woolsack's thought and time –
> Four times I hoped each pond and tree
> Enclosed, enclosed, enclosed to see –
> Yet thither the British Public comes,
> And townsfolk, 'scaped from smoky slums.
> Four times I sought, from fern and furze,
> To bar the children, maids and curs,
> But now success I hope to meet,
> And dance to the hisses at my feat:

> At an indignant people's voice,
> Whilst you may grumble, we'll rejoice,
> And nimbly, nimbly dance with *nil*
> To check us in my Father's Will.[11]

This was supported by an article headed 'The Hampstead Heath Monopolist':

> This Sir Thomas Wilson, who wants all the fodder on Hampstead Heath to himself, is, we understand, trying, for the fifth time, to get a Bill through the House of Lords, to enable him to enclose and build upon said Heath, reserved by his father's will as open country . . . Ought not Sir Thomas Wilson to be enclosed himself? Does he not deserve – having strayed from the paternal path – to be shut up in a pound, on a small allowance of hay, and no thistles?

When the Bill was debated in the House of Lords it was supported by the Earl of Wicklow and the Marquess of Clanricarde, both large landowners, while the opposition was led by the Earl of Shaftesbury, the reformer and philanthropist. This time it was defeated only by a narrow margin.

Encouraged by this, Sir Thomas tried again in 1854. He now sought power to build only on the Finchley Road estate, and placed an advertisement in *The Times* emphasising that the Bill did *not* apply to the East Park estate. This presented a problem for the Heath defenders: the Heath was not directly threatened, but if Sir Thomas succeeded in altering his father's will in this respect, thereby setting a precedent, it would later be more difficult to save the East Park. The Heath defenders therefore offered Sir Thomas a compromise, which had already been suggested on a previous occasion: they would not oppose the Bill if he would pledge himself not to build on the East Park estate in his lifetime. This deal offered Sir Thomas many advantages since he would have been left free to develop the great potential of the Finchley Road estate. This would, in any case, have taken the rest of his lifetime – he was 54 – and his heirs would have been free to develop the East Park estate after his death. Sir Thomas therefore had everything to gain and little to lose from this compromise, and a wiser man would have accepted the offer; but he rejected it, leaving the Heath defenders no choice

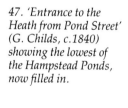

47. 'Entrance to the Heath from Pond Street' (G. Childs, c.1840) showing the lowest of the Hampstead Ponds, now filled in.

but to oppose the Bill.

After a lively debate the House of Lords passed the Bill. It was the first time since 1829 that Sir Thomas had got an Estate Bill through the Lords, but he was to receive short shrift from the Commons. London MPs were well aware of the importance of Hampstead Heath to their constituents and turned out in force to defeat the Bill by 97 votes to 43.

The Settled Estates Act

The dispute took a new and unexpected turn in 1855 when the government introduced the Leases and Sales of Settled Estates Bill. As we have seen, tenants-for-life under family settlements who wanted to acquire wider powers over the family estates had to obtain a special Act of Parliament for the purpose, unless they could agree with their heirs to alter the settlement. To save time and expense the government's new Bill provided that in future such applications should be dealt with by a Chancery judge instead of going before Parliament. When this Bill reached the House of Commons it was realised that, if it became law, it would enable Sir Thomas to ask a Chancery judge to overrule Parliament's rejection of his Estate Bills. Moreover the *public* would not be represented in the Chancery court, as it had been in the Lords and Commons, and Sir Thomas' chances of obtaining building powers would be greatly increased.

The Heath defenders had to move quickly. In Gurney Hoare's discussions with the London MPs it was decided that a clause must be added to the Bill excluding from its provisions any person who had previously applied to Parliament for extended powers and had been refused them. This was proposed by Sir John Shelley, the member for Westminster, but opposed by two lawyer MPs (Whiteside and Malins) who argued with some force that the exclusion would apply to only one individual and was therefore unfair and unconstitutional; because of this dispute the government decided to withdraw the Bill.

The following year the Bill was reintroduced and the same clause was proposed by Sir John Shelley; the clause was again opposed by Whiteside and Malins but was carried 'amidst great cheering' by 84 votes to 42. After a tussle with the House of Lords this clause became Section 21 of the Leases and Sales of Settled Estates Act 1856. Between 1857 and 1860 Whiteside and Malins (with the support of Sir Thomas) made three attempts to delete Section 21 from the Act, but on each occasion they were defeated by the London MPs, lobbied and briefed by Gurney Hoare.

[1] F. M. L. Thompson: *Hampstead: Building a Borough* (1974).

[2] Hansard 19 June 1829.

[3] *Morning Herald*, 18 May 1843.

[4] *Pictorial Times*, 27 May 1843.

[5] Letter of 2 August 1844 in the archives of the Hampstead Heath Protection Society (London Borough of Camden, Local History Collection).

[6] *The Times*, 14 October 1844.

[7] *The Times*, 4 September 1845.

[8] William Howitt: *The Northern Heights of London* (1869).

[9] *The Builder*, 2 July 1853.

[10] *Morning Herald*, 3 June 1853.

[11] *Punch*, 11 June 1853.

CHAPTER SIX

The Heath Preserved

In the early 1850s it became clear that the only sure way to protect the Heath and the adjoining lands was to purchase them for the public. Sir Thomas was held at bay for the moment but a new problem would arise after his death, when the Maryon Wilson property in Hampstead would go to his brother John. Unlike Sir Thomas his brother had a son of full age with whom he could agree to break the entail and grant building leases.

As we have seen, the difficulty about purchasing the Heath for the public was that the government felt that London should bear part of the cost but there was, at the time, no local authority in London which could raise the money. The great provincial cities had been given their corporations by the Municipal Corporations Act of 1835 but nothing had been done for London, largely because of the opposition of the City of London.

This situation was changed in 1855 by the Metropolis Management Act, which replaced the ancient parish vestries with elected vestries and created a new central body, the Metropolitan Board of Works, most of whose members were elected by the vestries. Although the Board's powers were limited, the Act created for the first time a body which could raise money from Londoners for the benefit of the capital. Instead of fighting a defensive battle against Sir Thomas and his estate Bills, it now became possible to think of acquiring the Heath and adjoining lands for the public.

A new initiative was launched by Thomas Turner, the effective leader of the Hampstead Vestry, and Hampstead's representative on the Metropolitan Board of Works. He and Gurney Hoare had worked together for some years in resisting Sir Thomas Wilson's Estate Bills and trying to persuade the government to accept the Cockerell plan. Turner now led the Hampstead Vestry in a two-year struggle to persuade the MBW to buy the Heath (together with East Park, Parliament Hill and Telegraph Hill) for the public. In February 1856 the Vestry approved a Memorial asking the MBW to take steps to purchase the Heath, and invited support from Marylebone, St Pancras and Paddington; but Turner met a setback in June, when the City of London representative moved and carried a resolution opposing this. He was unwilling to accept defeat, however, and early in 1857 he won the support of the Works and Improvements Committee of the MBW. This put him in a much stronger position and he renewed his pressure on the Board itself, which agreed to discuss the matter again in June. But at this stage Sir Thomas Wilson intervened. His solicitor, William Loaden, sent a letter to the Board in which he alleged that 'the expenditure of public money in the purchase of Hampstead Heath will be a fraud upon the public, until the lord of the manor . . . shall apply for an Act of Parliament to enclose the Heath'.[1] Loaden was asked to attend a meeting of the Board at which he assured them that 'the public need not fear any enclosure of the Heath till a Bill for that express purpose shall be brought forward'.[2]

The Board rather naively accepted this assurance (which, as we shall see, was not honoured) and decided not to pursue the matter; but Thomas Turner, an experienced lawyer, was not so trusting. His next step was to publish a 40-page pamphlet, *The Case of Hampstead Heath*, setting out in masterly style the legal and historical background and the case for public purchase. The Hampstead Vestry then made one more effort to promote the purchase, by-passing the MBW, and submitting their own Private Bill to Parliament.[3] This was a very ambitious step for a parish vestry and its success depended largely on the attitude of the MBW. In January 1858 Gurney Hoare headed a deputation from Hampstead to ask the MBW to support the Bill, but the Board decided to oppose it instead. In the event the Private Bill Committee of the House of Commons rejected it as going beyond the scope of a Private Bill; this marked the end of Turner's campaign.

Having defeated this attempt to purchase the Heath, Sir Thomas Wilson now took the offensive once more, this time with a change of tactics. Since losing his 1829 Bill he had directed his efforts to developing the two Maryon Wilson estates in Hampstead, and had not made any attempt to build on the Heath itself. But he now decided to make use of his manorial rights by threatening to build on the Heath, or disfigure it in other ways, if he was not allowed to develop his estates; from now on he used the Heath as a hostage, making frequent threats to despoil it.

In the summer of 1861 Sir Thomas began his offensive in the columns of the newly-founded *Hampstead Express*. Then, at the annual dinner for copyholders in December, his steward made a thinly-veiled threat that Sir Thomas would start building on the Heath if he were prevented from developing his estates. This produced the desired result when the *Hampstead Express* urged Gurney Hoare and his friends to withdraw their opposition to his building plans.[4] But Gurney Hoare, who was made of sterner stuff, responded by calling a public meeting in Hampstead in April 1862. Here he moved a resolution, which was carried unanimously, 'that if Sir T. M. Wilson should take steps for obtaining a private Act to grant building leases over his Finchley Road estate, and pledge himself not to seek further building powers, this meeting will not oppose such an application'. This was the compromise already offered to Sir Thomas, and he rejected it once again.[5]

Between 1862 and 1864 Sir Thomas made three more attempts to delete Section 21 of the Settled Estates Act, each time unsuccessfully. At the same time he exploited his manorial rights on the Heath by allowing increased excavation of sand and gravel, causing great damage to the trees, gorse and heather.

(Overleaf)
48. 'Road leading to North End' (G. Childs, c.1840) with the Gibbet Elms on the left.

C. CHILDS.

49. Cottages at North End (G. Childs, c.1840).

The Select Committee of 1865

The fight for Hampstead Heath was one of the first great conservation battles of modern times; previously it had been an isolated struggle but in the 1860s it became part of a wider campaign. As more and more of the open spaces near large towns were covered with houses, there was a growing recognition of the importance of preserving what remained. This took shape in a national campaign to save the commons from the lords of the manor who wanted to enclose and build on them.

The issue came to a head in 1864 over Wimbledon Common. The lord of the manor, whose intentions were honourable but misguided, proposed that one-third of the common should be sold and the proceeds used to drain and improve the remainder and turn it into a public park. He promoted a Private Bill in Parliament, but the scheme was strongly fought by the commoners and inhabitants. This dispute focused public attention on the threat to London's commons and in February 1865 the MP for Lambeth, Mr Doulton, urged the appointment of a Select Committee to enquire into the best means of preserving them for the public. The parliamentary debate which followed showed that many of London's MPs shared his views.

One of the best speeches was made by a young Liberal member, George Shaw-Lefevre, who was to make a major contribution to the preservation and extension of Hampstead Heath. Shaw-Lefevre (pronounced to rhyme with fever) was born into the world of high politics, his father being Clerk of the Parliaments and his uncle Speaker of the House of Commons. After

50. Cottages at Squires Mount (G. Childs, c.1840).

51. George Shaw-Lefevre.

(Photo Jeremy Marks/Woodmansterne)

qualifying as a barrister he was elected to Parliament as Liberal member for Reading, and in 1865 he was already well-known as a radical. He later became a Cabinet minister but his greatest contribution to public life was his long campaign to preserve open spaces; without his efforts many of the English commons and forests would have been enclosed and covered with houses.

The proposal to appoint a Select Committee was agreed; John Locke, MP for Southwark, was appointed chairman and Shaw-Lefevre was a member. Several witnesses gave evidence on the Hampstead Heath dispute, including Sir Thomas Wilson. This is the one occasion for which we have a verbatim record of his remarks and opinions, and it gives a vivid impression of the irascible baronet. John Locke was clearly hoping that Sir Thomas would be prepared to discuss a compromise over the Heath, but he was soon disillusioned. He asked Sir Thomas:

I understood that you wished to make some proposition with a view of settling the dispute about Hampstead Heath?

No, I have no proposition to make.

We were informed that you were willing to dedicate a certain portion to the public upon obtaining the right to build upon another part?

No, I make no compromise and no promise. In the year 1829, my intention was to have laid out Hampstead Heath with ornamental walks; but I lost my Bill for building on other parts of my property, and having always been thwarted, I must now see what I can do to turn the heath to account, and get what I can. By the outcry that has been made against me, I am deprived of about £50,000 a year. My

(Facing Page)

52. 'Keats listening to the nightingale on Hampstead Heath'. A posthumous portrait by Joseph Severn with the Firs Avenue in the background (c.1845).

53. Bank Holiday on Hampstead Heath (Phil May, 1899).

property would have produced me that without the slightest injury to the public, if any of my Bills had been passed.'

Locke then asked Sir Thomas to explain his plans for the Heath.

'Is there nothing that you wish to do with it now?'
'Only to turn it to account.
'What do you mean by turning it to account?'
'I might build an Agar Town there upon 21 years' lease.'

Agar Town was a notorious shanty town near Camden Town, and one of the worst slums in London. The Committee was clearly taken aback by this threat:

'Have you now any serious thought of converting the Finchley-road property, or the Hampstead Heath property, into an Agar Town?'
'It would depend upon circumstances; if I am not able to build upon my inclosed land, I shall build upon the uninclosed. There is no reason why I should make any further sacrifice.'

This led Locke to ask Sir Thomas whether he was seeking powers to build on the Heath itself:

'Have you ever, in any of the applications that you have made to Parliament, sought to convert Hampstead Heath proper to building purposes?'
'Not by Bill, because I apprehend I could do so without.'
'As regards your power of building upon the heath, you consider that you can do that without any Bill at all?'
'Of course I can, by granting or by taking land forcibly; and then who is the party to oppose me in anything I may do? If I build where the sand is dug out, who could interfere? There would be a great outcry, of course.'

Sir Thomas was then asked about the rights of the public:

'I suppose it is almost unnecessary to ask you; do you concede or believe that the public have any right upon Hampstead Heath?'
'I conceive that they have none whatever, any more than they have upon my property at Charlton.'

A little later he raised the subject of his father's will, perjuring himself again:

'A great deal has been said in former time about a clause in my father's will prohibiting building upon Hampstead Heath. That is perfectly absurd, and the only ground for such an assumption is that it is an entailed estate, and the law of the land prohibits a longer lease than 21 years, under such circumstances, without the assistance of Parliament. My father was very ill when Mr Lyddon came down to Charlton to add that codicil about the property at Woolwich and Charlton, and Mr Lyddon suggested that the same thing should be done with regard to Hampstead. My father said, "I am too tired now to do it; I must put it off until tomorrow."'

At the end of his evidence, the Committee again asked Sir Thomas about his rights on the Heath:

'Do you claim the right of inclosing the whole of the heath, leaving no part for public games?'
'If I were to inclose the whole of it, it would be for those only who are injured to find fault with me.'
'I suppose you would sell Hampstead Heath?'
'I have never dreamt of anything of the kind; but if the public chose to prevent me, or to make any bargain that I am not to inclose it, they must pay for the value

*54. The Sandy Heath
and the Firs Avenue
(1844).*

of what they take from me.'
    'Do you consider Hampstead Heath private property?'
    'Yes.'
    'To be paid for at the same rate as private land adjoining?'
    'Yes.'[6]

Sir Thomas' answers made it clear to all concerned that he regarded the
Heath as his private property; that he claimed the right to enclose and build
on any part of it; and that he was not prepared to make any kind of
compromise. When his evidence was published in the press he became even
more unpopular than he had been before. He seemed determined to play
the role of the wicked landlord of Victorian melodrama, and his opponents
naturally made full use of his blunt and tactless comments.

The evidence given to the Select Committee, which covered all the
London commons, revealed two strongly opposed views of the law on
common rights. Many lords of the manor argued that the rights of the
commoners had lapsed through disuse, while the public had no legal rights
at all; they, as landlords, were therefore free to enclose the commons if they
wished. But the commoners maintained that their rights were still valid and
enclosure would be illegal.

The Select Committee strongly supported the second view; their report
made two main recommendations. The first was the repeal of the medieval
Statute of Merton under which lords of the manor claimed the right to

enclose commons, but this recommendation was not accepted by the government. The second was that provision should be made for regulation schemes, under which individual commons could be properly managed, thus removing one of the main arguments for enclosure. This was accepted by the government and incorporated in the Metropolitan Commons Act of 1866. This gave the London commons a measure of protection but the failure to repeal the Statute of Merton left the lords of the manor with many of their powers, and the danger of piecemeal enclosure remained.

The publication of the Committee's report had immediate consequences. The lords of the manor, having failed to get the Committee to accept their view that they virtually owned the commons, took immediate steps to vindicate their claims. In Epping Forest hundreds of acres were fenced off and tree-felling began; the commons of Berkhamsted, Plumstead and Tooting were enclosed and others were threatened. If these enclosures had been left unchallenged most of the London commons would have been lost to the public.

The conservation group had to move quickly and Shaw-Lefevre took the lead; in the summer of 1865 he founded the Commons Preservation Society to organise resistance. As chairman he was supported by John Stuart Mill, Thomas Hughes, Leslie Stephen and others, while Hampstead was represented by Gurney Hoare and Philip Le Breton. The Society soon had plenty of work on its hands. As each common near London was threatened or enclosed, local residents formed committees, and opposition was organised with the Society's advice and assistance. The first of these battles came to a climax in Hampstead.

(Facing Page)

55. 'Caen Wood' by John Wootton, 1760.

56. The Engine House of the Hampstead Water Company (artist unknown).

57. Kenwood from the Lake (G. Shepheard, 1825).

(Overleaf)
58. The Sandy Heath showing the effect of sand-digging (1856). Spaniards Road is on the right.

91

59. London from Hampstead Heath (by an unknown artist, 1803).

The Heath in Danger

In his evidence to the Select Committee Sir Thomas said that if he were frustrated in his plans to build on the Maryon Wilson estates, he would 'consider the most profitable mode of building upon Hampstead Heath proper, or best way of converting it to my own profit'. His opportunity came in 1866 when the Midland Railway extended its line to the new terminus at St Pancras Station. The company required great quantities of sand and gravel, and Sir Thomas was able to sell it a large part of the surface of the Heath. The area excavated was the land on both sides of Spaniards Road, where the layer of Bagshot Sands was deepest. By 1867 thirty cartloads a day

60. 'Pond, Path and Anglers' 1971, oil on canvas, size 39½ × 39½. By Bryan Senior, b.1935.

(Overleaf)
61. A large sandpit near Spaniards Road (1867).

were being taken and some of the sandpits were 25 feet deep. Gorse, broom and heather were destroyed, trees were undermined, and the Sandy Heath was devastated so completely that it has never recovered. Sir Thomas also decided to exploit part of the East Park estate as a brick-field, and granted a 21-year lease to John Culverhouse, a Hampstead builder.

In 1865 and 1866 he promoted further Bills seeking power to build on the Finchley Road estate. Having once said that he would continue to promote Bills until Parliament got tired, this time he nearly succeeded. The 1866 Bill passed the House of Lords and was debated in the Commons on 9 July. Its supporters argued that it was no threat to the Heath since it empowered Sir Thomas only to build on the Finchley Road estate. The London MPs replied

*62. The Firs Avenue,
looking towards Harrow
(G. Barnard, 1850).*

that he had refused to give any pledge not to build on or near the Heath, and his proper course was to sell his manorial rights to the Metropolitan Board of Works. This Bill (Sir Thomas' fifteenth and last) was defeated by the narrow margin of 72 votes to 65.

Sir Thomas' response was to carry out his threat to build on the Heath itself, which he claimed the right to do as lord of the manor, and work started on two sites in November 1866. One of these was the summit of the Heath, next to the flagstaff near Whitestone Pond, where he began a new estate office, and the other was a site near Squires Mount. The alarm was sounded in a letter printed by *The Times*:

> Building has now actually commenced on the Heath. The first house is in course of erection by the lord of the manor at the flagstaff – the very point which commands the most magnificent of our views. Brick making is to be extended over a considerable portion of the Heath, and the rest is to be covered with cottages and huts; in fact another Agar or Kensal Town is to occupy this splendid site.[7]

By choosing the flagstaff site for his estate office Sir Thomas had deliberately thrown down the gauntlet. When his friend Henry Sharpe remonstrated with him he replied:

> I build the first house where everybody can see it, so that it may be known what I intend to do. A steam engine is at work in my wood here [Uckfield in Sussex]. More than a half [?] of fencing is already cut. Some of it is already at Hampstead and more will follow. If the Publick want the heath they may have it by paying for it. I find the mineral value is about ten thousand pounds per acre.[8]

Gurney Hoare now took control of the situation and consulted the Commons Preservation Society about the response to Sir Thomas Wilson's challenge. There were two choices. The first was to make an approach to Sir Thomas with a view to purchasing his manorial rights on the Heath. This was strongly opposed by the Commons Preservation Society; in their view it was pointless to try to negotiate with lords of the manor who regarded the commons as their private property, since the price demanded would be quite unrealistic. The second choice, which the Society favoured, was to challenge in the law courts Sir Thomas' claim to exclusive private ownership. The Society's solicitor had given much thought to the legal strategy; his advice was that one or more of the copyholders should bring a suit in Chancery against Sir Thomas Wilson, on behalf of the other copyholders, in order to establish their legal rights on the Heath.

Early in December Gurney Hoare called a meeting of leading members of the Heath defence group, and representatives of the Commons Preservation Society, at which it was decided to accept Sir Thomas' challenge. Gurney Hoare then wrote to him on 6 December:

Dear Sir,

My neighbours, as well as myself, much regret that you should have commenced building on the Heath. Several gentlemen interested in the matter met last night, and were advised that the only course open to them was an appeal to law.

I can assure you that they will do this with reluctance, as they have no hostile feelings towards you, and it would give great and general satisfaction in this place if you would consent to stay all proceedings, and to obtain a legal decision on the real or supposed rights of yourself and the copyholders, by an amicable suit. In this manner a long and costly litigation, as well as much irritation, may be avoided.

Believe me,
Your very obedient Servant,
J. Gurney Hoare.

Sir Thomas' reply was brusque, to say the least:

Sir,

Take your own course.
I am, Sir,
Your obedient Servant,
Thos. Maryon Wilson.[9]

Legal proceedings against Sir Thomas began on 10 December in the names of Gurney Hoare and two other copyholders. In the meantime Hampstead Vestry and the MBW were following a more conciliatory line. The Vestry sent a deputation to seek the help of the MBW, which decided 'that the Chairman be requested to seek an interview with Sir Thomas M. Wilson, and ascertain whether he is prepared to negotiate for the dedication of Hampstead Heath and adjoining lands to the public use'. The chairman, Sir John Thwaites, made his way to Charlton House and later submitted his report to the Board:

The Chairman reported that he distinctly stated to Sir Thomas, that, provided an arrangement could be come to between the Board and himself, for the purchase of the Heath, they would be willing to join him in an application to Parliament, for the purpose of obtaining the necessary powers to enable him to grant building leases of such portions of the adjoining lands as the Board might not require for

63. 'The People's Holiday' (1859).

the purposes of the public, and that in all probability, Parliament, having regard to the fact that such an arrangement would secure the Heath to the public in perpetuity, would accede to the request. Sir Thomas, however, did not appear disposed to agree with that suggestion, but argued that he saw no reason why he should sell his property at Hampstead for the purpose, as he alleged, of gratifying and benefiting certain parties, who had, for years, opposed him in obtaining his rights. Upon being urged again by the Chairman to favour him with his views as to the value of his interest in the Heath, Sir Thomas Wilson stated that, having regard to the price which he obtained for some land at Charlton, sold by him to the South Eastern Railway Company, he was of opinion that the property on Hampstead-heath was worth from £5000 to £10,000 per acre. The Chairman expressed his astonishment at the amount mentioned by Sir Thomas.[10]

And well he might, for Sir Thomas' figures, which would have valued his manorial rights at £1,250,000 to £2,500,000, were wildly inflated. In their evidence to the Select Committee of 1865 the Heath defenders valued the manorial rights at only £30 per acre. This may have been on the low side, but after Sir Thomas' death his brother was quite happy to settle for about £200 per acre, which was probably a generous price. The interview confirmed the hard-line view of the Commons Preservation Society that it was pointless to talk to Sir Thomas, since he was not interested in any reasonable settlement, and the Metropolitan Board decided to await the outcome of the lawsuit.

64. Hampstead Heath (John Leech, 1860).

There was another serious danger to the Heath in the 1860s. This was a time of frenzied railway development, and the railway companies found it easier and cheaper to take their lines through the commons than through private property. The commoners and inhabitants of the district concerned had no *locus standi* to appear before the Select Committee of the two Houses of Parliament, whose duty it was to consider the Private Bills submitted by the railway companies. The lords of the manor, on the other hand, were seldom concerned to protect their commons, and often welcomed the railway companies because of the compensation they received. This led to many of the London commons, including Wandsworth, Banstead, Tooting, Mitcham and Barnes, being badly cut up by railways at this time.

In 1866 alone there were no less than three schemes to build lines across Hampstead Heath. The North Metropolitan Railway proposed to make an open cutting, three-quarters of a mile long and·fifty feet deep, through the Heath from Hampstead Ponds to Golders Hill. The Metropolitan and St John's Wood Railway planned an extension to Finchley, crossing the Heath for about three-quarters of a mile, partly on an embankment and partly in cutting. The third scheme was a link line between the Great Western Railway at Southall and the London docks, again cutting across the Heath. A few years later another company proposed to drain the Highgate Ponds and lay a line along the bed of the valley with a tunnel under Kenwood.

Shaw-Lefevre and the Commons Preservation Society mounted a strong campaign against all these threats to the commons, and the schemes affecting Hampstead Heath were either defeated in Parliament or were not pursued for other reasons.

Hoare *v.* Wilson

When Sir Thomas Wilson heard that legal proceedings had been started he reacted angrily in a letter to Henry Sharpe: 'I have heard this morning and have received notice that Hoare and others *Have joined* in a Chancery suit against me. The object of this note is to tell you that it will prove a very expensive affair to those who may join it.'[11] The Heath defenders, well aware of this, set up the Hampstead Heath Protection Fund Committee to raise funds, with Gurney Hoare as chairman. Most of the committee members were Hampstead residents but the Commons Preservation Society was represented by Shaw-Lefevre and two other MPs. The case was of great importance to the Society, since it was clear that a series of major lawsuits would have to be fought in defence of the London commons, and Hampstead Heath was the first to come to court.

In January 1867 the committee issued an appeal for funds which received wide publicity and strong support. There is said to be a contemporary caricature of Gurney Hoare, mounted on a Hampstead donkey, marching to battle against the lord of the manor. Charles Dickens published an article in *All the Year Round*,[12] strongly supporting the Heath defenders, and *Punch* attacked Sir Thomas again in verse.[13]

Since the public had no legal standing, the only way to defend the Heath was to assert the rights of the copyholders. Gurney Hoare and the other copyholders claimed that they had been entitled 'from time immemorial' to pasture their cattle on the Heath; to cut heath and gorse for fodder and litter; to dig sand and gravel for their own use; and to use the Heath for enjoyment and recreation. If these common rights could be established they would of course mean that Sir Thomas was not undisputed master of the Heath as he claimed.

Sir Thomas for his part denied that the copyholders had any rights except that of pasturage, which applied to only three or four 'ancient copyholders'. Apart from this, he claimed complete freedom to 'destroy or otherwise deal with the pasture, heath, gorse, herbage and trees upon the said heath and to sell and carry away for his own profit the sand, gravel, loam and other like materials which form part of the soil of the said heath and to enclose and build upon the said heath'.

The case came up for hearing on 24 June 1868 before Lord Romilly, the Master of the Rolls, and lasted four days. Counsel for the Heath defenders was Sir Roundell Palmer QC, a distinguished lawyer who later became Lord Chancellor and carried through the major reform of the legal system in 1873. But Lord Romilly's judgement was something of an anti-climax, since he refused to give a ruling on the issues of fact involved in the case (i.e. what exactly were the customs of the manor) and directed that these issues should be tried by a common law judge before a special jury. This judgement was disappointing for the Heath defenders, who foresaw protracted litigation and heavy costs, but in May 1869 the situation took a new turn. As a member of the Hampstead Vestry put it, rather unkindly, 'the hopes of Hampstead people were brightened by the death of Sir Thomas Wilson'.

HAMPSTEAD : BUILDING THE BONFIRE ON THE HEATH.

65. 'Building the Bonfire on the Heath' (1863).

The Heath Acquired

After Sir Thomas' death the Maryon Wilson property in Hampstead, including the lordship of the manor, was inherited by his brother Sir John. Unlike Sir Thomas he was a friendly and reasonable man with whom it was possible to negotiate; having no wish to prolong the bitter and unnecessary dispute, he let it be known that he was willing to sell his manorial rights on the Heath. In January 1870 the Metropolitan Board of Works, on which Philip Le Breton represented Hampstead, opened negotiations; the Board made an initial offer of £25,000 but this was rejected, and after some hard bargaining agreement was reached on a price of £45,000 plus £2000 lawyers' and surveyors' costs.

The total area acquired was about 220 acres (see map on p. 105). The purchase required the authority of Parliament and the Hampstead Heath Act was passed in 1871. Section 12 provided that 'the Board shall for ever keep the Heath open, unenclosed and unbuilt on', and Section 16 read:

> The Board shall at all times preserve, as far as may be, the natural aspect and state of the Heath, and to that end shall protect the turf, gorse, heather, timber and other trees, shrubs and brushwood thereon.

The MBW decided to take formal possession of the Heath on Saturday 13 January 1872; members were due to meet at Hampstead Heath station and perambulate on foot the boundaries which had been marked out by flags. Unfortunately there was a heavy downpour of rain, so the perambulation was made by road in 'covered conveyances'. In a brief ceremony at the flagstaff, the Heath was dedicated by Colonel Hogg, the chairman of the Board, to the free use and recreation of the people for ever.

The long struggle to save the Heath had been brought to a triumphant conclusion, achieved by a powerful alliance of Hampstead residents, London MPs, reformers, conservationists and public opinion. But were the Heath defenders justified in frustrating Sir Thomas' building plans? In a recent book[14] Professor F. M. L. Thompson argues that during the greater part of the forty-year struggle Sir Thomas was not trying to build on the Heath itself but on the Maryon Wilson estates adjoining it. In his view Sir Thomas was shamefully treated by the Heath defenders, who had no right to prevent him covering his property with houses, if it was profitable for him to do so, just as any other landowner was at liberty to do.

But there were, as we have seen, special features about Sir Thomas Wilson's case which set it apart from those of other landowners. His plan to build on the East Park estate was a very real threat to the East Heath, which would have been surrounded by houses and dissected by several access roads. Whatever he may have thought, the Heath was not his private property. Moreover, under his father's will he was only tenant-for-life of the Hampstead estates and it was clearly his father's intention that they should not be built upon. Knowing that Parliament would be unwilling to override such a clear intention, Sir Thomas repeatedly perjured himself by saying that the inhibition on the Hampstead land was an oversight of his father's.

In judging Sir Thomas it is also worth noting that his efforts to develop his

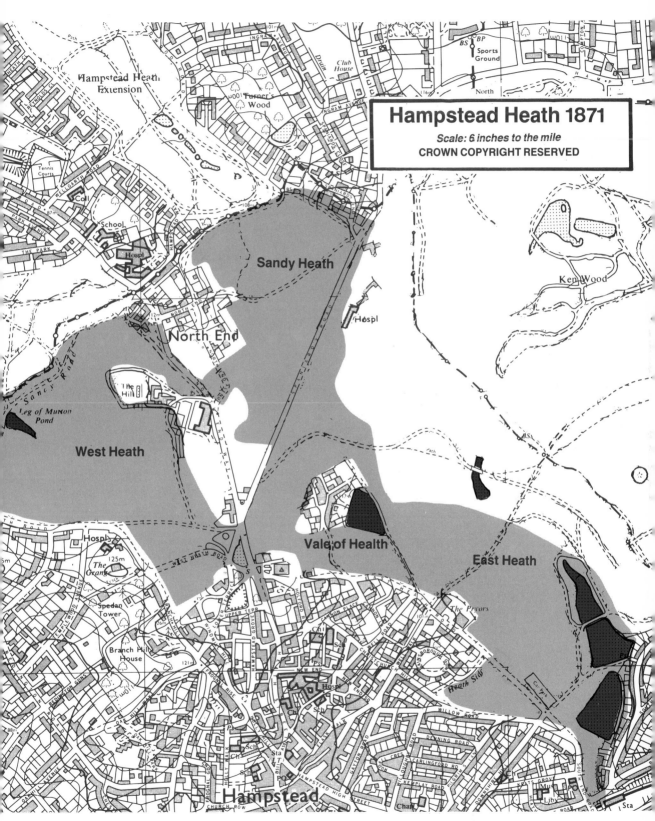

Hampstead Heath 1871

Scale: 6 inches to the mile
CROWN COPYRIGHT RESERVED

Sandy Heath

Ken Wood

North End

The Hill

Leg of Mutton Pond

West Heath

Vale of Health

East Heath

The Pryors

Heath Side

Hampstead Heath Extension

Turner's Wood

Club House

Sports Ground

Hospl

Hospl

Hospl

The Grange

Spedan Tower

Branch Hill House

Hampstead

private estates at the expense of the public were not limited to Hampstead. At Charlton, in Kent, he followed the same policy; but here he was in a stronger position, being the owner of Charlton House, chairman of the bench of magistrates and Deputy Lieutenant of Kent. He annexed a large slice of the village green, stopped up the highway in front of Charlton House, and then tried to enclose the rest of the green.[15] Here Sir Thomas rode roughshod over the opposition, but in Hampstead he faced stronger opponents.

Finally, Sir Thomas more than once rejected the sensible compromise offered by the Heath defenders, which would have allowed him to develop the valuable Finchley Road estate. In the words of his own agent he wanted 'the whole hog, bristles and all', and he paid the penalty for his obstinacy.

[1] MBW Minutes, 29 June 1857.

[2] Ibid.

[3] Minutes of Hampstead Vestry, 1857. (London Borough of Camden, Local History Collection).

[4] *Hampstead Express*, 25 December 1861, reprinted in a pamphlet *The Heath in Danger* (1862).

[5] *Hampstead Express*, 23 April 1862.

[6] Select Committee on Open Spaces (Metropolis), Report and Evidence, 1865.

[7] *The Times*, 28 November 1866.

[8] Letter dated 30 November 1866 in archives of Hampstead Heath Protection Society (London Borough of Camden, Local History Collection).

[9] F. E. Baines: *Records of the Manor, Parish and Borough of Hampstead* (1890).

[10] MBW Minutes, 1 February 1867.

[11] Letter dated 13 December 1866 in the archives of Hampstead Heath Protection Society (London Borough of Camden, Local History Collection).

[12] *All the Year Round*, 23 February 1867.

[13] *Punch*, 13 January 1867.

[14] F. M. L. Thompson: *Hampstead: Building a Borough* (1974).

[15] J. G. Smith: *History of Charlton* (1970).

CHAPTER SEVEN
'Appy 'Ampstead

When the Heath became public property in 1871 it was a scene of devastation. The effect of the sand-digging was vividly described by the *Illustrated London News* in September that year:

> The whole space on the summit of the hill, both to the right and the left of the high road which passes over it from Hampstead to Highgate, has been ruthlessly dug up for gravel or sand; an immense quantity of which has been carted away, leaving a dreary, desert prospect of hideous pits and shapeless heaps as far as the view extends over the hill itself, with a few miserable furze-bushes here and there, a ragged tuft of dusty ling, or some wretched weed content to grow in its degraded situation, but without one square yard of verdant turf for a baby to roll upon. The very body of the earth had been cut away to an amazing depth, with the entire surface of those parts of the Heath which formed the brow and the crown of the hill, as well on the north-west side, looking towards Hendon and Finchley, as on the side looking down the Vale of Health towards London. Holes are scooped out close to the high road thirty feet or forty feet deep, and big enough to bury the corpses of a nation for half a century, at the ordinary rate of mortality, but ugly enough to deter the boldest survivor from approaching so ghastly a spot.

In December *The Times* called on the Metropolitan Board to carry out a major programme of improvements and tree-planting, and to lay out the Heath as a park on the lines of Hampton Court, Kew Gardens and the parks of Capability Brown.[1] Fortunately Philip Le Breton was chairman of the Parks Committee of the MBW; he pointed out that the Hampstead Heath Act required the Board 'to preserve, as far as may be, the natural aspect and state of the Heath'. He described his policy as 'to repair the mischief which had been done by digging and removing sand and turf, to restore the herbage, fern, gorse, heather and broom, to plant judiciously, and generally endeavour to bring back the heath to the beautiful wild condition in which it was some years since'.

This policy was welcomed by the tight-fisted Metropolitan Board. An offer by an MP to present a thousand broom plants was gratefully accepted, a few labourers were employed to fill up some of the holes made by sand-digging, and furze, grass and other seeds were bought for sowing on the Heath. Bye-laws were approved and a Heath Constable was appointed at a wage of 20 shillings a week. Under this policy the Heath began to recover from the savage mauling of the 1860s. A few years later James Thorne noted in his *Handbook to the Environs of London*:

> The Board of Works have happily done little in the way of improvement, and nothing towards rendering the Heath prim or park-like. Under their 5 years of

ROTTEN ROW NORTH.

'Ampstead Carrier. "WOULD YOU BE SO KIND, MUM, AS TO FETCH 'IM A GOOD WHACK 'ITH YOUR RUMBERELLER?"

66. 'Rotten Row North'
(Charles Keene, 1865).

judicious neglect, Nature has begun to reassert her rights. The bare sands are becoming clothed with verdure; the banks, especially on the N., are purple with heather, the harebell is once more becoming common, the furze and broom have spread vigorously and bloomed abundantly, and the brake is everywhere fresh and flourishing. Hampstead Heath, in fact, looked better in the summer and autumn of 1875, than it had looked for the previous thirty years, and promises to look still better in the years that are to come.

The Hampstead Donkeys

In Victorian times one of the main activities of visitors to the Heath, both adults and children, was donkey- and pony-riding. Hampstead was famous for its donkeys and contemporary pictures show visitors careering about the Heath on donkeyback or riding along Spaniards Road in pony chaises.

The donkeys are first recorded in the 1820s although they probably arrived earlier. They were not welcomed by the citizens of Hampstead, and in July 1825 the Vestry discussed at length the 'nuisance occasioned by the placing for hire of pony chaises and donkies on the Heath, and other parts of the parish'. The Steward of the manor reported that he had taken counsel's opinion on the problem but was advised against prosecution. The Vestry

'earnestly requested' the Steward to impound any ponies or donkeys standing for hire on the Heath, but he evidently felt that he lacked the power to do this.

By the 1830s there were about a hundred donkeys standing for hire; they were pastured on the Heath and often strayed on to the village green near Whitestone Pond. Local residents complained to the Heath Keeper who asked the Steward for permission to 'pound' them:

> Aug 5, 1835 – Mr Jackson's complements to Mr Lyddon hoping will do something Not to suffer the horses and Donkeys to stand so ner his Premises as they Quite take the wole of the seat under the larg healme tree. Languige bad, Nusance great. May 21, 1836 – Not less than 100 Donkys on the Heath Dailey, som from Highgate, som from Camden Town and if not Pounded imposoble to keep off the green.[2]

Stevenson was not allowed to impound the donkeys, although he was told to make a census of their owners.

From 1850 onwards there are many descriptions and pictures of the cavalcade of donkeys and ponies on the Heath. Charles Dickens wrote that 'the donkey is truly the indigenous animal of Hampstead Heath' and another account described the whole Heath as 'one gay tournament'. Even Karl Marx, during family picnics on the Heath, used to entertain his children by riding a donkey. The donkeymen and their animals congregated on the Upper Heath near the Whitestone Pond, which George du Maurier called the Ponds Asinorum, and on the Lower Heath at the foot of Downshire Hill.

When the Heath became public property in 1871 the donkeymen, whose touting had become a nuisance, were brought under control and licensed. A

67. 'Hampstead Heath on a holiday' (1872).

(Overleaf)
68. 'Quiet Times: A Sketch on Hampstead Heath' (E. Buckman, 1873).

stand for 45 donkeys was made near the Vale of Health and another for 60 at the bottom of Downshire Hill. An offer from the Metropolitan Drinking Fountain and Cattle Trough Association to erect two granite troughs at the donkey stands, for £11 each, was accepted; the one near Downshire Hill is still standing. The Hampstead donkeys continued to flourish in the 1880s and 1890s but their popularity and numbers declined in the present century.

The Hampstead Heath Fair

In the middle of the nineteenth century the Heath offered only simple entertainments for visitors. A typical holiday outing is described in a popular music-hall song of the day, 'Hampstead is the Place to Ruralize'. It recounts the adventures of a large family party who set out for the Heath in several horse-vans, stopping for refreshments at the 'Load of Hay' in Haverstock Hill. They eventually reach the Heath and try their luck with the donkeys:

> The donkeys next we tried them,
> But scarce each animal stirs,
> Than those who tried to ride them
> Were kicked off among the furze.

At tea-time they make their way to the Vale of Health where they are provided with tea by the cottage people, only to find tadpoles in the tea and a large toad sitting in the tea-pot. The chorus runs:

> Oh! Hampstead is the place to ruralize,
> Ri-ti-turalize, extra-muralize,
> Hampstead is the place to ruralize
> On a summer's day.

But from about 1850 onwards the Hampstead Heath fair at Easter and Whitsun entertained the growing holiday crowds. Its origin is obscure. A fair at Flask Walk in Hampstead is recorded in the seventeenth and early eighteenth centuries, and another flourished for many years at West End until it became rowdy and was put down by the magistrates in 1820, but the fair on the Heath is a modern one which dates from the mid-nineteenth century.

(Facing Page)
69. 'Les Montagnes de Hampstead' (George du Maurier, 1876). Du Maurier lived in Hampstead and the large dog is Chang, his St. Bernard.

It started at South End Green, then known as Pond Street, the main gateway to the Heath from London, and there are reports of small fairs here in the 1830s. In 1835 the Heath Keeper recorded in his diary that he stopped a Whitsun fair on the green which then belonged to the lord of the manor: 'I stopt the fair at Pond Street, would not alow the Swings nor Stawles to stand on the Lord's ground.'

During the 1850s the Hampstead fair must have benefited from the closing of three famous London fairs – Bartholomew Fair in 1855, Camberwell in 1856 and Greenwich in 1857. But the real impetus was probably the opening of the Hampstead Junction Railway (which became the North London Line) in January 1860. The Hampstead Heath station at South End Green provided a direct route from the East End to Hampstead, bringing thousands of Londoners on summer weekends and holidays. By 1865 it was estimated that about 50,000 holidaymakers flocked to Hampstead Heath on a fine

LES MONTAGNES DE HAMPSTEAD.

Showing how we adventurous Inhabitants of the Hilly Suburbs of North London beguiled the weary Hours during the recent Snowy Weather.

Easter or Whitsun holiday.

The next move came from Sir Thomas Wilson, who was determined to exploit his manorial rights to the limit; in about 1865 he decided to regularise the fair and charge the stallholders for their pitches. He set aside a large area of the Lower Heath near Hampstead Ponds as a fairground. His action was noted by Charles Dickens' paper *All the Year Round:* 'The shows, too, which plant themselves down at Easter and such times, have been laid under contribution, and made to pay toll for the privilege of pitching on the Heath.'[3]

The Bank Holiday Act of 1871, which followed a campaign by Sir John Lubbock, gave another impetus to the fair. Easter and Whit Mondays, and the first Monday in August, were made Bank Holidays. Apart from Christmas, Boxing Day and Good Friday, these were the only holidays enjoyed by many working people and they made the most of them.

The following year a full report on 'Hampstead Heath on Whit Monday' with a large picture (Illustration 67) appeared in the *Illustrated London News*.[4] This makes it clear that the fair had already spread over the whole of the East Heath, stretching from South End Green to Spaniards Road and the Vale of Health. This whole area was a 'congregation of working-class Londoners, everywhere swarming in multitudinous clusters, like flies upon a batch of cakes in a baker's sunny shop-window.' The entertainments were largely organised by the crowds themselves. The most popular diversion was 'Kiss-in-the-Ring', followed by dancing 'effectively promoted by the presence of many Italian and English performers on the grinding organ'. The donkeys were ridden furiously but Spaniards Road was reserved for 'the cabs, the barouches and the chaises, which brought parties of middle-class spectators to watch the fun of the day'. There were also coconut shies, stereoscopes, skipping ropes, sweetmeat vendors, silhouette artists, and a machine with a 'galvanic battery' which gave an electric shock.

By the 1880s it was estimated that about 100,000 Londoners came to the Heath on a fine Bank Holiday, and the fairs had become famous. The factory girls from the East End, wearing long skirts and huge hats adorned with coloured feathers, danced with their coster menfolk on the Heath. The fair at 'Appy 'Ampstead became an important part of the East End way of life, like hop-picking in Kent. Indeed the Heath found its way into Cockney rhyming slang, in which Hampstead Heath (usually shortened to 'ampsteads or 'amps) means teeth.

The spirit of the fair was caught by a famous music-hall song of the early 1890s, written and sung by the coster-singer Albert Chevalier:

> Now if you want a 'igh old time
> Just take the tip from me,
> Why 'Ampstead, 'appy 'Ampstead is
> The place to 'ave a spree.
> You parker wiv dinarlies, an'
> I'm willin' for to bet,
> The day you spent on 'Ampstead 'Eath,
> You never will forget!
>
> Oh, 'Ampstead! 'appy, 'appy, 'Ampstead,
> All the doners look so nice,

Talk about a par*i*dise,
Oh, 'Ampstead's very 'ard to beat,
If you want a beano it's a fair old treat!

Bank 'oliday's the time of course
    To see it at its best,
Wiv blokes and doners by the score
    All very neatly dressed.
Sich ikey 'ats an' feathers, green,
    Red, yeller, pink and blue;
An' coves in roun'-my-'ouses all
    Cut very saucy, too!
    Oh, 'Ampstead, etc.

The toffs may talk of Rotting Row,
    There ain't no place on earth
Like 'Ampstead, 'appy 'Ampstead, for
    To get yer money's worth.
The blokes as owns the cocoa-nuts,
'Twont break yer to support,
Three shies a penny's wot I calls
    A fine old English sport.
    Oh, 'Ampstead, etc.

(*Parker wiv dinarlies*, pay your money; *doner*, woman or girl; *ikey*, smart; *roun'-my-'ouses*, trousers.)

The local newspaper provides a detailed account of the fair on Easter Monday, 1884:

This favourite 'Northern Height' was visited by an enormous concourse of Holiday-makers on Monday, who poured on to the Heath until late in the afternoon, and probably numbered altogether not far short of 100,000 people. They came from all parts by road, rail, omnibus, and by the tramcars which run to the verge of the parish, near the Kentish-town entrance to Hampstead-heath. Fair-like amusements were provided in abundance by industrious folk from the East-end and elsewhere, who had very early in the morning taken up their positions on the Heath: and even before reaching Hampstead-heath those who came from Kentish-town by way of Gospel-oak found swings and a novel roundabout, the latter worked by steam, and with cars fitted up as sailing boats, whose motion they imitated, ready to claim a share of their patronage. The roadway running up the Lower Heath from the railway station on towards the Vale-of-health and the Upper Heath was densely crowded. On the Heath skirted by this roadway there was a continuous line of stalls and barrows, at which toys, ices, tea and coffee, stewed eels, baked potatoes, etc., could be obtained; while gambling for bottles of scent, walking sticks, coconuts, and other prizes was going on briskly at various spots. 'Ladies' tormentors', as usual, were sending forth their liquid streams on various parts of the Heath, especially where the crowds were greatest, while pony and donkey riding were as popular as ever, together with skipping, the performances of conjurors, the 'try-your-strength' machines etc. Bands of music, surrounded by throngs of merry dancers, were hard at work, and open-air preachers were met with. The Vale-of-health was crowded, the tea-gardens, swings, and steam roundabouts, with similar amusements to those found on the Lower Heath, attracting thousands of visitors. The Upper Heath, also, presented a lively scene, the pond on the summit forming a 'beat' round which pony and donkey-riders galloped from morning till night. The West-heath, with its gorse and furze-bushes just breaking out in golden beauty, also attracted a large number of the holiday-makers, though the great mass of the people did not trouble to travel so far as this point for their day's fun.[5]

The holiday scene on Hampstead Heath attracted the famous humorous

70. 'Oh, 'Ampstead,
'Appy 'Appy
'Ampstead;' (Phil May,
1894).

71. The North London Railway (1900 poster).

(Overleaf)
72. The Suburban Hotel, later the Vale of Health Tavern (c.1864).

COMPANY LIMITED.

VALE OF HEALTH IN THE CENTRE OF HAMPSTEAD HEATH.

SUBURBAN HOTEL COMPY LIMITED.

73. Hampstead Heath near the Vale of Health (c.1907).

artists of Victorian times. John Leech and Charles Keene recorded the enthusiastic donkey-riders and their reluctant mounts, while the Cockney Bank Holiday carnival was captured by Phil May; George du Maurier's drawings show the more sedate recreations of the middle classes.

On one occasion the sheer size of the crowds led to disaster. On Easter Monday, 1892, while crowds were enjoying themselves on the Heath the weather suddenly broke. Rain and sleet started to fall and thousands surged towards Hampstead Heath station. As they pressed into the building they were trapped, struggling and screaming, on the steep staircase to the platforms. By the time the crowd had been dispersed two women and six boys had been crushed to death.

The Vale of Health

The holiday crowds and fairs led to the transformation of the Vale of Health. In 1851 it was still a very small hamlet: the census of that year records five houses, a dozen cottages and the old parish almshouses. On summer weekends and holidays the cottages provided tea-making facilities after the donkey-rides. William Howitt described the scene:

ON HAMPSTEAD HEATH.

I. SKIPPING. II. ACROBATS. III. THE VALE OF HEALTH. IV. LOST CHILDREN'S TENT. V. AMBULANCE TENT.

74. On Hampstead Heath (from G. R. Sims: Living London, *1902).*

> In front of a row of cottages, and under the shade of willows, were set out long tables for tea, where many hundreds, at a trifling cost, partook of a homely and exhilarating refreshment. There families could take their own tea and bread and butter, and have water boiled for them, and table accommodation found for them, for a few pence.[6]

But this idyllic scene was too good to last. Under the Copyhold Enfranchisement Act of 1852, copyholders were able to purchase the freehold of their land compulsorily from the lord of the manor; they could then build on the land and reap the full benefit of development themselves, instead of paying increased 'fines' to the lord of the manor. A West Hampstead landowner and property developer, Donald Nicoll, was quick to take advantage of this change by purchasing some copyhold land in the Vale and acquiring the freehold. He then formed the Suburban Hotel Company which built a large hotel close to the pond; by 1864 it was advertising its tavern and tea gardens with accommodation for two thousand people.

This hotel, later known as the Vale of Health Tavern, was a prominent edifice with a large and dominating tower. The building was widely criticised and William Howitt complained of 'a monster public-house with a lofty tower and flag, to attract the attention of Sunday strollers on the Heath. Of all places, this raised its Tower of Babel bulk in that formerly quiet spot, the Vale of Health.'[7]

Donald Nicoll also built several houses on his land. His example was followed by other copyholders and the Vale of Health grew rapidly: the number of houses increased from 17 in 1861 to 41 in 1881. Since there was no possibility of expanding over the Heath, the houses were built close together on the existing plots, and the Georgian cottages were flanked by Victorian terraces. The result was considered to be an eyesore, and in April 1886 the *Illustrated London News* complained of 'that detestable modern hamlet in the hole styled the "Vale of Health" . . . where a huddle of paltry new small houses, a monstrous tavern, built in the castellated style, with dismal tea gardens, noisy dancing platforms, and painted swinging machines . . . deface the spot in which Keats and Shelley listened to the nightingale'.

[1] *The Times*, 12 December 1871.
[2] The Heath Keeper's Diary (London Borough of Camden, Local History Collection).
[3] *All the Year Round*, 23 February 1867.
[4] *Illustrated London News*, 25 May 1872.
[5] *Hampstead and Highgate Express*, 19 April 1884.
[6] William Howitt: *The Northern Heights of London* (1869).
[7] Ibid.

CHAPTER EIGHT
The Heath Expands

Sir John Maryon Wilson, who inherited the two Hampstead estates on his brother's death in 1869, was subject to his father's will like Sir Thomas, but he had a son and heir with whom he could agree to break the entail and grant building leases. Fortunately he decided to develop the Finchley Road estate first, leaving the East Park estate, and in 1875 work began on Fitzjohns Avenue, which followed an earlier footpath across the Conduit Fields. At the same time development started on the western part of this estate with the construction of Priory Road, Canfield Gardens and Broadhurst Gardens.

Meanwhile the East Park estate, from the Viaduct Pond down to the Hampstead Ponds, was still being ravaged by brick-making. The soil was part of the Claygate Beds, the intermediate layer between the Bagshot Sands and the London Clay. As early as 1844 Sir Thomas had found that it provided good brick-clay, and the bricks for the Viaduct itself had been made in a small brick-kiln near the pond.

In 1865 or 1866, having finally given up the idea of building on the East Park, Sir Thomas decided to exploit it as a brickfield. He leased the lower part of the estate for 21 years to John Culverhouse, a Hampstead builder, 'by whom it was cut down, chopped and carved in a manner utterly destructive of its natural form, which was that of a hill gracefully swelling with a fine outline, while the very pretty avenue of trees, at the public footpath from Hampstead to Highgate, was ruthlessly despoiled'.[1]

An old photograph (Illustration 75) shows that the brickworks and brickmakers' cottages were in the field below the Viaduct Pond. The strip of land from there to the Hampstead Ponds, on both sides of Sir Thomas Wilson's road through the estate, was dug up for brick-clay. The results can be seen today in the excavated area which is now a football field on one side of the road, and in the steep banks and beds of nettles on the other. The whole area is shown on the 1871 Ordnance Survey map as the Brickfields.

By the 1880s the East Park was ripe for building development and Culverhouse's lease was due to expire. There was clearly a danger that Sir Spencer Wilson, who succeeded his father Sir John in 1876, would decide to build when the lease fell in. The local paper printed some correspondence about the need to protect both the East Park and Parliament Hill, which belonged to the fourth Earl of Mansfield, but nothing was done until Shaw-Lefevre, on a visit to Hampstead, realised the growing threat.

On his initiative a public meeting was held in January 1884 in the Hollybush

75. *The Brickfield on East Park estate (c.1880).*

Assembly Rooms at Hampstead. It was organised by Edward Maurice, the son of F. D. Maurice, the Christian Socialist, and the Commons Preservation Society was represented by Robert Hunter (later Sir Robert), Shaw-Lefevre's right-hand man. The meeting was attended by well-known Hampstead figures such as F. E. Baines, Professor Hales and G. W. Potter, and a committee was elected 'to ascertain the opinion of the neighbourhood as to the expediency and possibility of securing additional open land on the borders of Hampstead Heath'.

The purchase of East Park and Parliament Hill was bound to be a very difficult and expensive operation. Unlike the Heath itself, these lands were private property and would command a full building price running into hundreds of thousands of pounds – the equivalent of several millions in today's money. To raise funds on this scale required a major national campaign and Shaw-Lefevre, who was now a senior Liberal politician, took over the operation himself. Early in 1884 a strong committee was formed with the aim of extending the Heath and preserving Parliament Hill; the Duke of Westminster was chairman with Shaw-Lefevre as his deputy and a galaxy of peers and politicians as members. The actual work was done by an executive committee under Shaw-Lefevre, including Octavia Hill, the housing reformer, and Robert Hunter, later co-founders of the National Trust.

The first step was to have preliminary talks with the two landowners – Sir Spencer Wilson for East Park and Lord Mansfield for Parliament Hill. It was essential that negotiations were conducted in tandem, since if one property was bought first the other would increase in value. The difficulty was that Sir Spencer wanted to develop East Park, or at least realise its value, while Lord Mansfield was reluctant to sell Parliament Hill in his lifetime. Eventually Sir Spencer was persuaded to suspend the sale of East Park and Lord Mansfield agreed to consider an offer for his land.

With the ground prepared in this way, it was hoped that the Metropolitan Board of Works would undertake the actual purchase. To win support, and demonstrate the importance and beauty of the site, a thousand guests were invited to a garden party on Parliament Hill in July 1885. The land to be bought was marked out with red flags and the guests were entertained in large marquees. The campaign received widespread publicity: a pamphlet was issued, *A Plea for the Extension of Hampstead Heath and the Preservation of Parliament Fields*, and pictures of the garden party appeared on the front pages of the *Illustrated London News* and *The Graphic*. *Punch* supported the campaign in doggerel verse:

> The M.P.'s assembled on Parliament Hill,
> At a swell Garden Party conducted with skill.
> 'Eh? Parliament, M.P.'s and Party? Oh dear!'
> Sighs the reader, 'I thought Dissolution was near.'
> *Mr Punch* sympathises, but begs to explain
> That this Parliament wasn't St. Stephen's again,
> And that men sick of *that* may extend their most hearty
> Approval to *this* – unpolitical – Party.
> For you see SHAW-LEFEVRE and BRAMWELL, and LLOYD,
> BURDETT-COUTTS, BODKIN, HUBBARD, and BRYCE were employed,
> Not in Party slang-whanging, such bricks quite beneath,
> But in scheming extension to old Hampstead Heath.
> The Parliament Fields and the Heath Park Estate,
> If saved from the Ogres of brick, tile, and slate,
> May be added thereto, if the price we'll afford,
> And can stir up that slow Metropolitan Board.
> *Mr Punch* thinks if this be *not* done, more's the pity.
> He'll do what he can do to help the Committee,
> And holds that the people should leave nothing undone
> To gain – whilst we can gain – a new lung for London.
> He'd like, in long streets close and weary to tramp, 'stead,
> More green bosky acres adorning old Hampstead.
> All lovers of Nature and friends of 'the childer'
> Should back SHAW-LEFEVRE in baffling the Builder![2]

The MBW was due to take its decision at the end of October, and a press campaign was launched in advance of this. Letters from Octavia Hill and Baroness Burdett-Coutts, the wealthy philanthropist who lived at Holly Lodge, Highgate, appeared in *The Times*, which also made a strong appeal to the Board in an editorial.[3] But the Board decided to take no action because of the very large sum of money involved, which it estimated at £350,000. This was a major setback which forced Shaw-Lefevre and his committee to revise their plans.

76. Octavia Hill.

The committee took the view that the MBW had over-estimated the cost of the purchase, which they put at about £300,000; they decided to try to get £50,000 from the St Pancras and Hampstead Vestries and a further £50,000 from the City of London Parochial Charities, leaving only £200,000 to be met by the Board. They introduced a Bill in Parliament on these lines, authorising the Board to acquire the land if it so wished, and this became law as the Hampstead Heath Enlargement Act, 1886. At the same time the committee conducted negotiations with the two landowners. Sir Spencer Wilson agreed to sell the 60 acres of East Park for £94,000 plus £1500 costs, and Lord Mansfield agreed on £200,000 for the 201 acres of Parliament Hill Fields and part of the Elms Estate.

By August 1887 the committee had established that the total cost of the purchase would not exceed £305,000, and had been promised £100,000 by the two vestries and the London Parochial Charities. They therefore asked the MBW to contribute the balance. To their dismay the Board offered a maximum of half the total purchase price – £152,500 – leaving over £50,000 still to find. A public appeal was then launched and Octavia Hill wrote to *The Times*:[4]

> I know these fields well, and how on bright summer Sundays and Saturday afternoons hundreds go to gather buttercups, see the hay made, to watch the sun set and the moon rise. I have seen the heath black like an anthill on a Bank Holiday, and I ask would it not be a privilege to help to increase its area by adding these great undulating fields? . . . The opportunity comes to this generation, and so far as we can see, it can never come again.

The money was raised and contracts were finally exchanged in March 1889. This purchase meant that Parliament Hill with its magnificent panorama of London, and a large surrounding area, were added to the Heath, increasing its size from 220 to 481 acres (see map on pp. 142/3). The whole operation had taken some five years to carry through. Most of the credit for this achievement must go to Shaw-Lefevre whose determination and resourcefulness finally carried the day; Parliament Hill is his monument.

77. Garden party held on Parliament Hill during the campaign to extend the Heath (1885).

'Boadicea's Grave'

One of the features of Parliament Hill is the 'tumulus', now covered with trees, which stands a little to the south of the footpath from Well Walk to Merton Lane. The origin of this mound is one of the unsolved puzzles of the Heath, and was the subject of much discussion and speculation during the campaign to purchase Parliament Hill. Despite its name and legend, the mound is certainly not Boadicea's grave.

According to another local legend the mound was the site of an ancient battle between two British tribes, one based in London and one in St Albans, and it contained 'the dust of the slain'. This theory had some support from Professor Hales, a historian and Hampstead resident, who gave an imaginative account of the battle:

> Looking at the lie of the country from the southern hill, we might suppose that the invaders had advanced from the north through the dip between the Hampstead and Highgate hills, and so entered the Valley of the Fleet, and were making for

London, when the Londoners, marching up that valley, met them at this spot, and dyed the stream with their own and their enemies' blood. Standing on the barrow, and looking north, one may picture very well the rush of those fiery Britons down the slopes, and the hand-to-hand encounter in the valley.[5]

It was decided to test these romantic legends by excavating the site, and this was done by Sir Hercules Read in 1894. No trace of any burial was discovered, and it was found that a large quantity of additional material had been added to the mound in recent times. Despite this negative result Sir Hercules came to the rather surprising conclusion that the tumulus was 'very probably an ancient British burial mound of the early-bronze period', a view discounted by later archaeologists.

The whole issue was re-opened in 1968 when the Museum of London acquired some previously unpublished drawings by William Stukeley, the eighteenth-century antiquary. One of these, dated 1 May 1725, shows a shallow, flat-topped mound surrounded by a ditch with a view of London and St Paul's in the background (Illustration 78). The mound is marked *Immanuentii tumulus* and Stukeley's caption reads:

This is a *tumulus* on an eminence by Caenwood, which I drew out on Mayday 1725, whether we always went a Simpling, in the years I lived in Town formerly. Dr. Wilmore now of Chelsea and Botanic professor in Apothecarys garden, commonly with me. It was the tumulus of some ancient Brittish king before Christianity: probably enough, of Immanuence monarch here just before Caesar's invasion.

78. The 'tumulus' on Parliament Hill (drawn by William Stukeley, 1725).

It appears from this that Stukeley, who had a fertile imagination and remarkable self-confidence, may have been responsible for the local legend

Immanuentii tumulus.

1.1. May 1725

that the site was an ancient burial mound. However, his drawing did serve to re-open the question of its origin.

A careful study of the map of Kenwood made in the sixteenth century throws some new light on this problem. There is no sign of the tumulus in the map, and the area where it now stands is clearly shown as part of the woodland. Kenwood is considered by botanists to be an ancient woodland, and was probably part of the great forest which covered most of the land north of London until Roman times. It is therefore an unlikely site for a Bronze Age barrow. Moreover, if the earthwork had been covered by woodland for a thousand years or more it would have suffered severe damage from the roots of trees, whereas Stukeley's drawing shows a tidy and well-defined mound and ditch. It seems more likely that the mound was made in the seventeenth century, possibly for a windmill, after the woodland had been cleared.

The 1894 excavation showed that a great deal of additional material had been added to the mound, which accounts for the fact that it is now much larger than Stukeley's mound. Why and when was this done? According to a local tradition the mound was built up and planted with Scotch pines in the late eighteenth century 'to form a picturesque object in the landscape',[6] and this is probably the explanation.

79. The 'tumulus' in 1889.

Protecting the Heath

In 1889 the London County Council replaced the Metropolitan Board of Works and took over responsibility for the Heath, Parliament Hill and East Park. The Council got off to a bad start. On taking over the East Park it immediately started to convert the attractive footpath from Well Walk to Merton Lane into a public road. At the same time it began to widen and extend the road made by Sir Thomas Wilson, which was disused and overgrown with grass, and covered both roads with black cinders.

This led to an outcry in Hampstead. Cards bearing the slogan 'Save the meadow paths' were put in shop windows, petitions against the roads were prepared, and angry letters appeared in the local paper. In a letter headed 'Vandalism at Hampstead', published in the *Daily Graphic*, Octavia Hill wrote:

> The late Metropolitan Board, in deference to popular feeling, left Hampstead Heath unfenced, and in the main wild and undisturbed. Cannot our new representatives realise in time that they will earn the gratitude of Londoners by doing the same with this great trust handed over to them? Cannot they understand that what people who go as far as Hampstead seek is, not the formality of the London park, not the wide roads, not the kerbstones, not the gas-lamps, not the levelled footpaths, but something of a freer space, where the wild flowers and meadow slopes may be seen in their natural condition?[7]

The Council's first reaction was to argue that new roads were needed across the Heath. The reason for making them so quickly was that, in clearing the brickfields, 'an immense quantity of cinders were found, and the only thing to do with them was to repair and make the paths'. This curious argument led to renewed protests, and eventually the Council saw reason and withdrew the plan.

But it continued with its policy of tidying up the Heath and making it more park-like. Another storm blew up in 1896 when a local artist organised a petition against the 'cutting and burning of old gorse bushes, the filling of hollows in paths with sand taken from banks and knolls, the drying up of small ponds by throwing in ashes, mud etc.' He collected an impressive array of signatures including those of Sir John Millais, George du Maurier, Norman Shaw and Herbert Beerbohm Tree. Another petition was presented to the Council by a Hampstead deputation which added a further complaint about indiscriminate and insensitive tree-planting along the Spaniards Road. These protests were supported by Sir Walter Besant, the novelist and historian of London, who wrote bitterly:

> The London County Council are certainly doing their best to secure the love and respect and gratitude of the people whose city they are protecting. Their attempt to convert the greater part of Hampstead Heath into a smug little Park like that of Victoria or Southwark; their grubbing up and cutting down of the venerable old gorse which had been the joy of artists for generations; their planting all about the place trees which do not belong to a Heath – these things have gone a long way to endear the Council to all Hampstead people.[8]

This dispute led to a meeting in April 1897 at which the Hampstead Heath Protection Society was formed 'for the protection of Hampstead Heath and the preservation of its natural beauties'. Since its formation the Society has fought many battles to protect the Heath, and it is still flourishing today as the Heath and Old Hampstead Society.

Golders Hill

In 1897 Golders Hill, a large mansion with a 36-acre park adjoining the West Heath, came on to the market. Barratt says that in the eighteenth century this estate belonged to Jeremiah Dyson, a friend of the poet Mark Akenside, but it has now been established that Dyson lived on the other side of North End Road. The Golders Hill estate was created in the 1760s by Charles Dingley, a colourful resident of North End who had made a large fortune through various enterprising and sometimes shady projects. These included building a sugar-beet refinery in Russia, erecting a mechanical sawmill in Limehouse and helping to finance the New Road from Paddington via Marylebone to Islington.

Dingley also had political ambitions, and worked hard to ingratiate himself with William Pitt the elder. Anxious to encourage Pitt to live in North End, he converted his own house into a mansion (later known as Pitt House) in which Pitt lived during his serious illness in 1767. In the meantime Dingley set about making a new estate for himself at Golders Hill. However, his enjoyment of this property was short-lived since his political ambitions brought him into conflict with the redoubtable John Wilkes. In 1768 Wilkes was elected one of the MPs for Middlesex, but was subsequently expelled from the House of Commons. A further election was held in 1769 and the Government persuaded Dingley, a strong opponent of Wilkes, to stand

80. Golders Hill Park (c.1905). The Victorian mansion was destroyed in the last war.

706   HAMPSTEAD. — Golders Hill. — The Mansion. — LL.

against him, but when Dingley made his way to the Brentford hustings a violent mob of Wilkes supporters prevented his nomination; during the fracas Dingley was seriously injured and he died a few months later.[9]

The landscaping of Golders Hill was carried out by John Coore, a later owner of the estate. He consulted Humphry Repton, who recorded that Coore 'asked for my advice at his villa in Hampstead where he retreated from business to enjoy the happiness of the society of his blooming wife and the possession of a blooming garden'.

The last owner of Golders Hill was an eminent surgeon, Sir Spencer Wells, after whose death it was put up for auction in 1897. At this time there was a boom in suburban flat-building and large blocks of mansion flats were being built in Hampstead. There was a real danger that, in the words of an eloquent contributor to the local paper, Golders Hill would be overlaid by 'mountainous monstrosities of glaring red brick such as now line the sides of the once-beautiful Finchley Road nearby, befouling the earth beneath, levelling the lovely trees, shutting out the free-blowing health-laden breeze, and loading the bright sky above with soot-laden smoke from thousands of reeking chimneys'.

Fortunately the bidding at the auction failed to reach the reserve price and the property was withdrawn. Efforts were then made to buy the estate and add it to the Heath, but they came to nothing and a further auction was arranged in June 1898. A few days before this a final effort was made by a local resident, Samuel Figgis, who called a meeting at his house in North End. It was decided to set up a guarantee fund to save the estate and the principal guarantors agreed to bid up to £35,000 at the auction; one of them was Thomas Barratt, author of *The Annals of Hampstead*, who was also chairman of A. & F. Pears, the soap company.

At the auction the speculative builders bid strongly and the price soon passed the £35,000 level. At this point the representative of the guarantors stopped bidding but the situation was saved by Thomas Barratt, who continued on his own account. The estate was knocked down to him at £38,000 and he resold it to the committee of guarantors at this price. Sir Henry Harben, the leader of Hampstead Vestry, then launched a campaign to raise the money: a meeting was held at the Mansion House with the Lord Mayor presiding, and 10,000 people came to a garden party in the grounds of Golders Hill. Within a month the money was raised and the park was opened to the public in December 1898.

The Tunnel under the Heath

The last decade of the nineteenth century saw the opening of several tube railways in London. One of the early projects was that of the Charing Cross, Euston and Hampstead Railway Company, which obtained the authority of Parliament in 1893 to build a tube railway from Charing Cross to Heath Street, Hampstead. But the company had difficulty in getting financial backing and no construction work was carried out.

The situation was then transformed by the arrival in London of Charles Tyson Yerkes, a freebooting American entrepreneur who had already had a spectacular career promoting and building tramway systems in Philadelphia

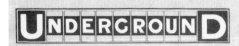

*81. Underground
Railway poster (1914).*

HAMPSTEAD

TAKE YOUR SON AND HEIR
WHERE THERE IS SUN AND AIR

WE CARRY DOGS AND FOLDING MAILCARTS.

SUNDAYS CHEAP RETURN FARE

4ᴅ

and Chicago. In the course of his activities Yerkes had been forced into bankruptcy, spent seven months in prison, given large bribes to city aldermen, and made a fortune of several million dollars. In 1899 he sold his Chicago interests and moved to London; the following year his syndicate bought the Charing Cross, Euston and Hampstead Railway Company. Building had not yet started, and Yerkes decided to extend the projected line from Hampstead to Golders Green to allow more room for the terminus. According to one account, after his agents had drawn up a plan for the extension Yerkes prospected the route himself with H. C. Davis, the vice-chairman. It was a wet day but when they arrived at Jack Straw's Castle the sun came out. Yerkes asked 'Where's London?', and on being shown the panorama below him he said, 'Davis, I'll make this railway.'

The extension to Golders Green required Parliamentary authority, and a Bill was presented to Parliament with plans showing a tunnel under the Heath. This caused immediate alarm in Hampstead. *The Times* published an article by a correspondent on 'The Tunnel under Hampstead Heath', expressing concern on two counts. The first was a groundless alarm about the effect on the Heath's vegetation:

> A great tube laid under the Heath will, of course, act as a drain; and it is quite likely that the grass and gorse and trees on the Heath will suffer from the loss of moisture . . . Moreover, it seems to be established beyond question that the trains passing along these deep-laid tubes shake the earth to its surface, and the constant jar and quiver will probably have a serious effect upon the trees in the neighbourhood by loosening their roots.[10]

A more justified cause of concern were the intermediate stations to be built between Hampstead and Golders Green, probably at Jack Straw's Castle and North End, and their effect on the Heath. A committee to oppose the Bill was set up with Samuel Figgis as chairman and Lord Mansfield as president. In January 1901, after a protest meeting at Hampstead Town Hall attended by 500 people, a petition was prepared opposing the Bill and suggesting an alternative route through Childs Hill.

The company's engineers replied with a statement answering the more exaggerated fears. There was no danger of draining the Heath since the tunnels would be deep in the London Clay, 150 feet below the surface, and there would be little vibration since multiple-unit trains would be used rather than locomotives. But the opposition scored a major victory when the company dropped the proposal for a station at Jack Straw's Castle, and agreed not to build any intermediate station in the borough of Hampstead. Having obtained this concession the Hampstead Borough Council withdrew its opposition, and although the Hampstead Heath Protection Society continued to oppose the Bill it became law in 1902. Tunnelling began in 1903 and the new line was opened by Lloyd George in 1907.

One of the Company's early posters showed a picture of the Heath and invited Londoners to 'take your son and heir where there is sun and air'. The cheap return fare on Sundays was fourpence. By 1910 it was estimated that about 300,000 people came to the Heath on a fine Bank Holiday.

The Heath Extension

The next addition to the Heath was largely the personal achievement of Henrietta Barnett (later Dame Henrietta), a remarkable woman who began her career of social work as one of Octavia Hill's assistants. When she married Samuel Barnett (later Canon Barnett) they decided to work in the East End; he became vicar of St Jude's, Whitechapel, one of the most deprived parishes in London. In 1889 they took Heath End House, near the Spaniards, as a weekend retreat and to provide extra accommodation for their activities. The house, which they renamed St Jude's Cottage, had a magnificent view across the Sandy Heath and Wyldes Farm to the open country beyond.

But all this was threatened by the Hampstead tube company, whose plans included a station at North End next to Wyldes Farm. This was just outside the Hampstead boundary, so it was not in breach of the company's undertaking to Hampstead Borough Council, but Mrs Barnett was horrified when she heard of it. As she wrote some years later:

> It would result in the ruin of the sylvan restfulness of that portion of the most beautiful open space near London. The trains would also bring the builder, and it required no imagination to see the rows of ugly villas such as disfigure Willesden and most of the suburbs of London, in the foreground of that far-reaching and far-famed view. Therefore there was nothing else to do but enlarge the heath.[11]

A woman of formidable energy and determination, Henrietta Barnett proceeded to form the Hampstead Heath Extension Council in the summer of 1903, with Sir Robert Hunter as her chief advisor and Shaw-Lefevre (soon to become Lord Eversley) as President. The Council's aim was to purchase eighty acres of Wyldes Farm adjoining the Sandy Heath and add them to the Heath.

Wyldes Farm had an interesting history. In medieval times the estate was the property of the Leper Hospital of St James, which stood on the site now occupied by St James' Palace. According to a tradition quoted by John Stow, the hospital was founded by the citizens of London 'before the time of any man's memory, for fourteen sisters, maidens, that were leprouse, living chastly and honestly in divine service'. The 'Spital for Leprous Maydes' gradually acquired large estates in London, given or bequeathed to it by pious Londoners; among these were two estates in the Hampstead area, Chalcotts (later Chalk Farm) and Wyldes.

But the wealth of the leprous maidens attracted the interest of the Crown, and when Henry VI founded Eton College he endowed it with the perpetual custody of the hospital. Henry VIII, however, decided that the site of the hospital would be an excellent location for the new royal manor house that he wanted to build near Whitehall Palace. In 1531 he acquired the hospital from Eton in exchange for some inferior estates in Kent and Suffolk, demolished it and built St James' Palace there; Eton was allowed to retain Chalcotts and Wyldes.

In the early nineteenth century Wyldes was let to John Collins, a small dairy farmer who scratched his name on one of the farmhouse windows – 'J. Collins, cow keeper and dairyman, North End'. To make a little extra

*82. Samuel and
Henrietta Barnett.*

money he extended the farmhouse and let out some rooms, one of the first tenants being the painter John Linnell. Charles Dickens also lived here for several weeks in 1837 when he and his wife were prostrated by the death of her young sister Mary Hogarth.

The Wyldes estate therefore belonged to Eton College, and the Heath Extension Council obtained an option from the College Trustees to buy eighty acres of it for £48,000. They hoped that the London County Council would contribute half this sum and that the balance would come from borough councils and private subscriptions. Despite a leader in *The Times* and a flow of private donations, the local authorities were less forthcoming. It was essential that Hampstead Borough Council should give handsomely, both on its own account and as a guarantee of local interest. There was strong opposition in Hampstead but the Council eventually agreed to give a disappointing £5000. The London County Council was even more reluctant; at first it declined altogether, but finally gave £8000 – a long way short of the hoped-for £24,000.

Henrietta Barnett then hit on the idea of altering the shape of the land to be acquired so as to give Eton College more building land fronting on to the new open space. This enabled the College Trustees to reduce the price to £36,000, and by the summer of 1904 the money raised was within £5000 of this figure. But this sum was hard to raise and only the work of Thomas Barratt, who organised a group of wealthy friends to guarantee the balance, enabled the Council to complete the purchase in time.

In the course of the struggle Henrietta Barnett had the idea of buying the remaining 240 acres of the Wyldes Estate to build a garden suburb, which eventually took shape as Hampstead Garden Suburb. Another unexpected result of her campaign was that the tube station at North End, opposite Wyldes Farm, was never built, for the creation of the Heath Extension in addition to Golders Hill Park meant that there were not enough local residents to make the station economic. By then the underground platforms had been built, however, and they can still be seen on the way to Golders Green.

[1] *Illustrated London News*, 3 November 1888.

[2] *Punch*, 8 August 1885.

[3] *The Times*, 28, 29, 30 October 1885.

[4] *The Times*, 9 November 1887.

[5] *Athenaeum*, 17 November 1883.

[6] Article by Professor W. Hales in *The Gentleman's Magazine*, April 1887.

[7] *Daily Graphic*, 31 January 1890.

[8] *The Queen*, 20 February 1897.

[9] Article by Philip Venning in *Hampstead and Highgate Express*, 19 May 1978.

[10] *The Times*, 25 December 1900.

[11] Henrietta Barnett: *Life of Canon Barnett* (1918).

CHAPTER NINE

The Saving of Kenwood

In the eighteenth century Kenwood played its part in history. It was the home of the Earl of Bute and the great Lord Mansfield, important figures in the world of politics, and it narrowly escaped being burnt down in the Gordon Riots. But in the nineteenth century the Mansfields played little part in public affairs, spending most of their time at Scone Palace, the family seat in Scotland.

Kenwood had a brief moment of glory in July 1835 when the third Earl of Mansfield entertained William IV and Queen Adelaide on a royal visit. A rather fulsome description appeared in the *Morning Herald*:

> Upon their Majesties arrival, the band of the Coldstream Guards struck up 'God Save the King'. The Royal Party proceeded to the fine terrace in front of the mansion, commanding a view of the beautiful grounds, wood and lake, where they received the homage of the numerous and distinguished party invited to meet their Majesties . . .
> The whole suite of noble rooms on the ground floor, 13 in number, were thrown open. The Royal table was in the principal dining room, where covers were laid for 34. It presented a display of rich plateaux and elegant service of plate. The Music Room, Green Room and Conservatory were also appropriated to the *déjeuner*, to which the company sat down shortly after six o'clock. The fine band of the Coldstream Guards performed a variety of beautiful music during the repast.
> As dusk approached the whole of the grounds in front of the mansion, the lake, bridge, and many of the trees, were illuminated with many thousand variegated lamps, producing a most enchanting effect. A large marquee was erected on the western lawn by Mr B. Edgington, and was appropriated to dancing, which commenced with several beautiful quadrilles by Weippert's fine band. The festive scene was kept up till late, and nothing could exceed the polite attention of the Noble host and hostess and the members of their family.[1]

The Marchioness of Salisbury, who was one of the guests, was less impressed by the occasion. She recorded in her diary that 'the grounds are excessively pretty, and if there had been enough to eat, it would have been perfect . . . The King and Queen and all the Royalties seemed extremely well pleased: the King in particular trotted about with Lord M. in the most active manner, and made innumerable speeches!'[2]

Another event was a *fête champêtre*, given by the fourth Earl in 1843, which was attended by Prince Albert. Apart from such occasions, with the Mansfields mainly in Scotland, Kenwood was closed for most of the year. But this had its advantages. While the Heath became more and more popular in the nineteenth century, and lost much of its wildlife and flora, Kenwood was closed to the public and became a kind of nature reserve.

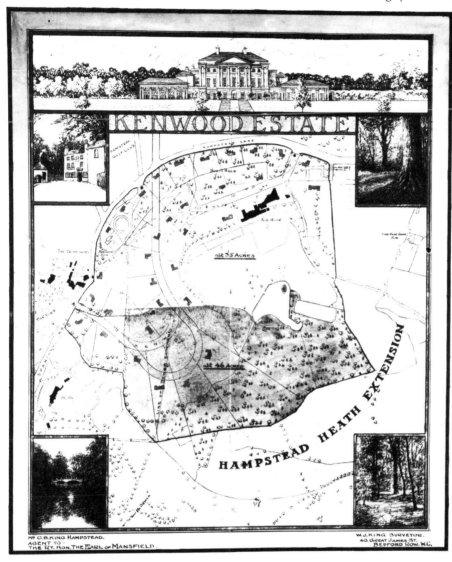

83. Lord Mansfield's plan for villas on the Kenwood estate (c.1923).

Kingfishers were often seen around the ponds and badgers had a sett in the wood, where the staff had instructions not to disturb them. Under one of the beeches was a patch of the very rare May Lily which grew in only one other place in England.

The neighbouring landlords took advantage of the growing demand for building land to develop their estates, but the Mansfields kept Kenwood as farmland. They also did all they could to preserve the adjoining land from being built upon. As we have seen, in 1789 they bought Millfield Farm, which had been advertised as suitable for villa development, and land in the Gospel Oak area was added later. When Lord Erskine, their neighbour at Evergreen Hill near the Spaniards, got into financial difficulties, they bought his land on the edge of the Heath; from 1829 onwards they strongly opposed Sir Thomas Maryon Wilson's efforts to build on the East Park estate.

When the Fitzroy Park estate was sold by the Southampton family in 1840 most of it was lotted for villas in large plots, but the land on the Kenwood boundary, on the Highgate side of Millfield Lane, was marked for terrace housing. The object was probably to force the Mansfields to buy this land in order to protect Kenwood, which they duly did; it was added to the Kenwood estate and now forms the north-east corner of the Heath.

By keeping Kenwood as farmland, and preventing building on its borders, the Mansfields ensured the preservation of the land which later became the eastern part of the Heath. But the sixth Earl, who succeeded to the title in 1906, lived wholly in Scotland and had little interest in Kenwood. From 1909 to 1917 the house was let to the Grand Duke Michael of Russia, in exile after a morganatic marriage. He and his wife took an active part in the glamorous social life of the time and entertained lavishly at Kenwood; he also made a cricket field and golf course in the grounds.

In the early summer of 1914 the Commons Preservation Society learnt that Lord Mansfield had decided to sell Kenwood for immediate building development. The estate amounted to over 200 acres, including the house and garden, the North and South Woods, the two lakes, three of the Highgate Ponds, and farmland leased to the Express Dairy Company. The Society made enquiries and found that a contract had already been prepared to sell the entire estate to a syndicate which proposed to develop the property by granting building leases. The 83-year-old Shaw-Lefevre (now Lord Eversley) convened a conference of local residents and conservation societies to consider what should be done. Lord Mansfield was reminded of a promise, made some years earlier, that the Metropolitan Public Gardens Association would be given the first opportunity of acquiring the property if he decided to sell it. He then agreed to postpone the sale, and offered instead to sell the estate to the public for £550,000, at which point the outbreak of war put a stop to any further negotiations.

During the war Sir Arthur Crosfield, the wealthy businessman and sportsman who built Witanhurst, the Highgate mansion overlooking the Heath, became interested in the acquisition of Kenwood, possibly as a national war memorial. In 1918 he and Lawrence Chubb of the Commons Preservation Society asked Lord Mansfield for an option to purchase the entire property for £220,000. This was rejected, but in the subsequent negotiations the original asking price of £550,000 was gradually reduced. Meanwhile the *Daily Telegraph* published several articles advocating purchase for the public, which were followed by a letter from Lord Eversley urging the formation of a national committee to raise the money:

> If I had the same strength and life that were mine when Parliament Hill was saved I would gladly throw-myself, heart and soul, into any movement for carrying out your suggestion that Kenwood should now be saved . . . Owing to the infirmities of age I am now unable to head or have a leading part in any such movements, but I trust that steps may be at once taken to form a strong and representative committee to deal with the matter.[3]

The Kenwood Preservation Council was then set up, with Sir Arthur Crosfield as chairman, and agreement was reached with Lord Mansfield on a purchase price of £340,000. Early in 1921 an appeal was launched and garden parties were held at Kenwood to raise funds. Substantial contributions were promised by the local boroughs but donations from the public were disappointing, and only £85,000 was raised.

In view of this response the Preservation Council adopted a less ambitious plan of buying only the meadow south of the wood and the fields on the Highgate side of Millfield Lane. The total area amounted to 100 acres, which Lord Mansfield agreed to sell at £1350 per acre, and the money was raised in 1922. On the advice of the officials of the London County Council, nine outlying acres near Fitzroy Park were resold to owners of adjoining land subject to a covenant that they should never be built upon. Another effort was then made to buy the wood itself and Lord Mansfield agreed to sell a further 32 acres, including the woodland and the two lakes, at £1000 per acre. These two separate purchases were vested in the London County Council and opened to the public in 1925.

But Kenwood House itself, and the 75 acres of parkland around it, were still in danger. The contents of the house, including the original furniture designed by Robert Adam for the first Lord Mansfield, had been sold at auction in 1922. The house itself was an empty shell, and Lord Mansfield's surveyors prepared a plan showing the estate divided into plots for 33 villas served by a new road, Kenwood Drive, through the middle of the park (Illustration 83). The Preservation Council had come to the end of its resources and it seemed that nothing could be done to save Kenwood.

At this point Edward Cecil Guinness, the first Earl of Iveagh, a wealthy businessman and public benefactor, came to the rescue. In 1925 he bought Kenwood and its grounds for £107,900 and arranged that they should become public property on his death. After furnishing the house and installing his valuable collection of pictures, Lord Iveagh died in 1927. His generous bequest, adding more land and a magnificent Georgian mansion to the Heath, was opened to the public in 1928.

[1] *Morning Herald,* 24 July 1835.
[2] M. C. Borer, *Hampstead and Highgate* (1976).
[3] Quoted in *Hampstead and Highgate Express,* 9 August 1919.

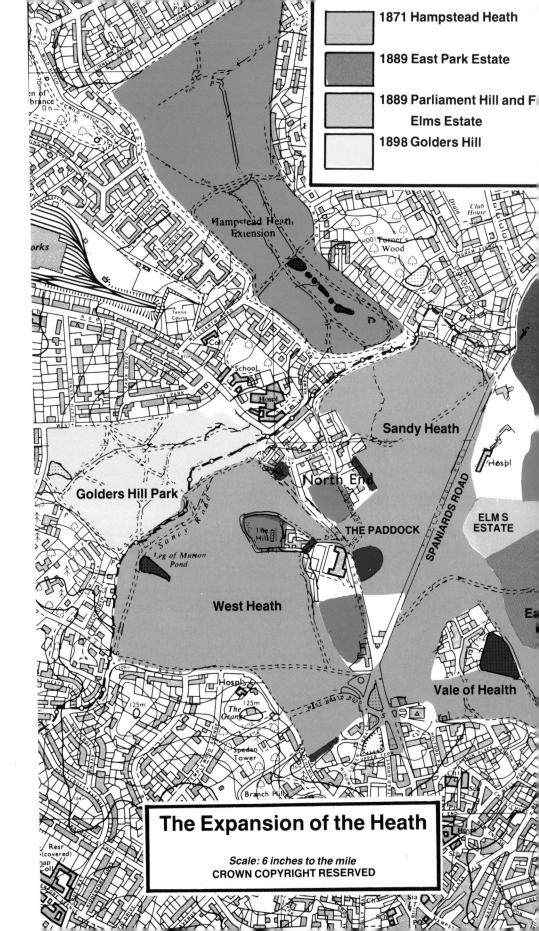

1871 Hampstead Heath

1889 East Park Estate

**1889 Parliament Hill and F[...]
Elms Estate**

1898 Golders Hill

Hampstead Heath Extension

Golders Hill Park

Sandy Heath

North End

THE PADDOCK

ELMS ESTATE

West Heath

Vale of Health

The Expansion of the Heath

Scale: 6 inches to the mile
CROWN COPYRIGHT RESERVED

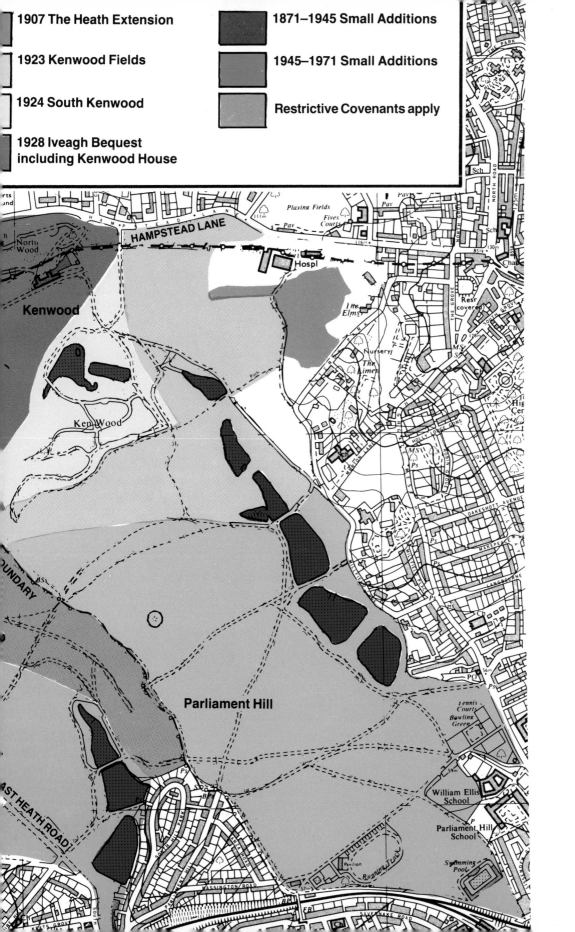

Legend

- 1907 The Heath Extension
- 1923 Kenwood Fields
- 1924 South Kenwood
- 1928 Iveagh Bequest including Kenwood House
- 1871–1945 Small Additions
- 1945–1971 Small Additions
- Restrictive Covenants apply

Kenwood

HAMPSTEAD LANE

Parliament Hill

143

CHAPTER TEN

The Heath Today

The need to fill sandbags at the beginning of the last war brought sandpits back to the Heath: one enormous pit was dug near the upper fairground above the Vale of Health, and another on the Sandy Heath near Heath House. Later they were filled in with rubble from London bomb-sites. In 1941 a parachute mine demolished the mansion in Golders Hill Park, while another destroyed several houses at Heath Brow north of Jack Straw's Castle, and part of the inn itself.

In the 1950s several small, but important, additions were made to the Heath by the LCC, with the help of vigorous local campaigns. Two bombed sites at Heath Brow were acquired in 1948 and 1951. Pitt House in North End Avenue, the mansion built by Charles Dingley for the elder Pitt, had to be demolished but its garden was acquired in 1954. In 1953 The Elms, a large Victorian mansion in Spaniards Road with extensive grounds, came on to the market for development; fortunately it was taken over as a hospital and three acres of the grounds were added to the Heath. A few years later the LCC bought The Hill garden, which had once belonged to Mrs Lessingham's Heath Lodge, and this was opened to the public in 1963.

The 1960s saw a tussle over the toll house at Spaniards Inn, which Finchley Council wanted to demolish since it obstructed the flow of traffic. Hampstead Council and the Heath and Old Hampstead Society strongly opposed this, and St Pancras Council and the brewers who owned the building were caught up in the dispute. Eventually the toll house was given to the Greater London Council, which had by then replaced the LCC, and it was added to the Heath.

In 1965 outline planning permission was given for houses to be built in the grounds of Witanhurst, the Highgate mansion overlooking the Heath. But in the years that followed there was a growing realisation that the fringes of the Heath would be irreparably damaged if houses were built on this lovely wooded slope, and determined opposition to the scheme was organised by the Hampstead and Highgate conservation societies. After a seventeen-year battle, a petition signed by 18,000 people and a public enquiry, the Department of the Environment allowed a modified scheme to go ahead. This was not the developers' last throw, however, for in recent months they have published proposals for a much larger number of houses to be built on the site.

This brings our history of the Heath up to the present day, but to complete the picture we must put on our walking shoes and look at the landscape itself. In this final chapter we shall take three walks round the Heath and study its history on the ground.

Walk One – The East Heath and East Park

South End Green, where we start this walk, is one of the oldest parts of Hampstead. There was a hamlet here in Tudor times, and probably before, known as Pond Street – a name that appears in the manor rolls in 1607. The name came from a small round pond which was filled in and replaced by the green in about 1835.

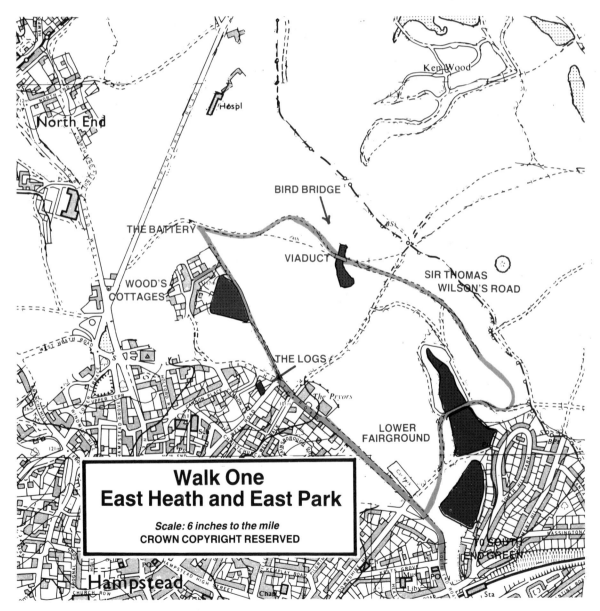

**Walk One
East Heath and East Park**

Scale: 6 inches to the mile
CROWN COPYRIGHT RESERVED

In the eighteenth century Pond Street was a fashionable part of Hampstead and it is no accident that it features in several of Chatelain's engravings. In the early nineteenth century, as we can see from a print of 1828 (Illustration 84), the little hamlet was still quiet and peaceful. On the south side of the green, where the Classic Cinema now stands, was Hereford House, apparently given to a Colonel Crump for his services in the Napoleonic wars. On the east side stood the White Horse, an eighteenth-century inn since rebuilt, and another large house, Clifton House. Next to this, on the site now occupied by South End Close flats, was Pickett's or South End Farm.[1]

But this tranquillity was not to last, for South End Green became the main gateway to the Heath for the thousands of Londoners who came to the holiday fairs. In 1860 the arrival of the railway destroyed some of the old houses and separated the green from the Heath. But the final blow came in 1886 when the London Street Tramway Company was allowed to bring its horse trams to South End Green, and a roadway 40 feet wide was cut across it for their benefit.

Beyond the railway station we come to the road, Parliament Hill, leading to South Hill Park. This area was once part of the Belsize Park Estate but was cut off from the rest of the estate when the railway was built. The land belonged to one Thomas Rhodes, who decided to develop it, and the streets and houses were built in the 1870s. At first sight it seems surprising that the Heath defenders did not protest against this housing development so close to the Heath, but we must remember that it started about 1870 when the Heath struggle was at its height and they had little time or energy to spare for anything else.

Walking up South End Road we pass a grassy paddock on the right opposite the foot of Keats Grove. This was once the lowest of the four Hampstead Ponds; in 1892 it was filled in after complaints by local residents that it had become polluted. The lowest of the three remaining ponds is reserved for wildfowl, which show their appreciation by gathering in large numbers. A pair of Canada Geese produces a family of goslings every year, and herons can sometimes be seen on the wooded bank. In the 1830s the Hampstead Water Company sank a well between the two lowest ponds to increase the supply of water to Kentish Town and Camden Town. A steam pumping engine was installed, housed in an octagonal pepperpot tower; this engine house remained a landmark for many years until it was demolished by the Metropolitan Water Board in 1907.

Further up South End Road, which becomes East Heath Road, we come to the site of the fairground on the right. As we have seen, the fairs started in the mid-nineteenth century and the fairground was laid out by Sir Thomas Maryon Wilson in the 1860s; the Lower Fair is still held here at Bank Holiday times. Just beyond the fairground is the horse-trough erected in 1872 for the Hampstead donkeys.

Over to our left, the present boundary of the Heath is Willow Road, but when the 1680 map was made the Heath extended a little further and the boundary followed a stream which ran just behind the present houses in Willow Road. This brook, a branch of the Fleet River, flowed from its source

84. *South End Green, then known as Pond Street (1828). The view is due east and Parliament Hill can be seen behind the houses on the left.*

85. *South End Road (c.1905). The old engine house can be seen in the centre.*

near Flask Walk to join the other Hampstead brook at South End Green, and in the nineteenth century there were watercress beds near the foot of Downshire Hill. The stream still flows underground and caused serious problems when the Freemasons' Arms in Downshire Hill was being rebuilt in the 1930s.

We follow East Heath Road up the hill to The Pryors, two large blocks of flats built on the site of a house owned by the Pryor family, a well-known Hampstead family related to the Hoares. The sandy road beyond The Pryors is the old roadway across the Heath to Highgate, which the London County Council tried to make into a public road until they were stopped by the protests of Octavia Hill and others.

On the left is Well Walk which led to the old Hampstead Wells. The Wells area was once part of the Heath, but in 1698 the Hon. Susannah Noel gave the chalybeate spring and six acres of the Heath to trustees for the benefit of the poor of Hampstead. The original pump-room stood on the south side of Well Walk and its gardens are now Gainsborough Gardens. Another assembly room was built later, on the other side of the road near Burgh House, but both have been demolished. Burgh House itself was the home of Dr Gibbons, the resident physician of Hampstead Wells; Foley House, on the corner of Well Walk and East Heath Road, may have been built by John Duffield, the speculator who leased the land and built the first pump-room.

Many centuries earlier, this area was known to the Romans. In 1774 a Roman burial was found near Well Walk, consisting of several urns, pottery and lamps, and in 1882 two Roman coins were found nearby on the Heath. These finds do not necessarily indicate a Roman settlement but they certainly suggest that at least one minor Roman road ran across the Heath.

A little further on, at the corner of East Heath Road and Well Road, is a large Victorian mansion called The Logs. Although it stands on the west of East Heath Road the land was once part of the Heath, and was in fact one of the two sites where Sir Thomas Maryon Wilson started building in 1866. The Logs, built in 1868, is described by Pevsner as 'a formidable atrocity', with 'yellow, red and black bricks, excrescences in all directions, arches pointed and round, motifs Gothic and Frenchified'.[2]

Here we leave the main road, taking the sandy track which forks off to the right. This brings us to the Vale of Health Pond, and the track runs along the top of the containing dam. In the steep valley on the right the Hampstead stream of the Fleet river runs down to Hampstead Ponds. Further on we come to a brick wall on the right, made by Sir Thomas Wilson in the 1840s to mark the boundary of the East Park estate; the attractive little pepperpot hut at the end of the wall was probably built at the same time.

The Vale of Health itself is a fascinating jumble of cottages and winding lanes. As we have seen, it owes its origin to the Hampstead Water Company which drained the swampy hollow and made the pond in 1777. The site did not attract the gentry, who preferred to build their houses on higher and drier land with open views, and the early inhabitants of the Vale were humbler people such as the parish poor, laundry-women, squatters and the village sweep.

The most famous of the early residents was Leigh Hunt, who lived here from 1815 to 1817 and made it the centre of his literary circle. There has been

THE VALE OF HEALTH. HAMPSTEAD HEATH (Photographed from an Aeroplane.)

86. The Vale of Health (an aerial photograph c.1907).

much confusion about the cottage in which he lived, mainly because a careful study by E. E. Newton, one of the most reliable of Hampstead historians, has been overlooked.[3] Newton's researches established beyond doubt that Hunt rented one of Woods' Cottages, a row of weather-boarded dwellings built by William Woods for letting to summer visitors. Woods' Cottages are in the centre of F. J. Sarjent's 1804 picture of the Vale (Illustration 17). Two of them (Hunt Cottage and Woodbine Cottage) are still standing, but the one rented by Leigh Hunt was probably the cottage pulled down some years later and replaced by South Villa. When Hunt returned to the Vale in 1821 he lived in a different house, probably the present Vale Lodge.

The 1860s saw the start of a second wave of building in the Vale. Most of the new houses were ugly Victorian terraces but the Villas-on-the-Heath are a notable exception; four of these, facing up the main road, are built in an unusual and attractive style with high gables. They were designed by a Mr Culverhouse, probably the builder who developed the brickfield on the East Park estate; he lived in one of the villas himself and the design is said to have been inspired by houses he had seen in Bavaria.

In addition to the Vale of Health Tavern a second hotel was built in the 1860s, but this was not a success and the building had a varied career, being used successively as a factory, lecture room, club, banqueting hall, Salvation Army hall, Anglo-German club and a warehouse. It was finally demolished in 1958 and a small block of flats built on the site. The Vale of Health Tavern was pulled down in 1964 and replaced by flats named after the painter Stanley Spencer, who once lived on the top floor of the tavern. The small fair on the land near these flats is run by the Grays, an old fairground family who bought the Tavern in 1920.

The local legend that the Vale of Health acquired its name in 1665, when it was a refuge for Londoners fleeing from the Great Plague, is of course unfounded: at that time it was an uninhabited swamp. In the eighteenth

149

HAMPSTEAD. VIADUCT AND POND.

87. Viaduct Pond, c.1905.

century the area was known as Hatches Bottom, and the name 'Vale of Health' is first recorded in 1801. Its origin is unknown but the probable explanation is that, as more cottages were built, Hatches Bottom seemed an unfortunate name and a more elegant one was chosen.

From the fairground a steep asphalt path climbs up the hill and brings us out on a broad, sandy roadway. On the left is the land known as the Battery where the Loyal Hampstead Volunteers had their exercise ground; today the Upper Fair is held here on Bank Holidays. Turning right along the sandy road we enter the old East Park estate which Sir Thomas Wilson tried so hard to cover with villas; this road was to be the central avenue of his estate, and beside it are acacias and other ornamental trees which he planted.

The track takes us to the Viaduct, built by Sir Thomas to carry his road across a swampy valley. The ornamental pond made by damming the stream is covered with yellow water-lilies in summer. The tumbled ground around the pond marks the site of the brickworks made by John Culverhouse when Sir Thomas granted him a lease on the lower part of the estate. The path on the left leads to the Bird Bridge, built at the same time as the Viaduct and now a favourite place for birdwatchers.

A little further on the road crosses the old track to Highgate, with an avenue of limes planted by the London County Council in 1905. Here we are standing in the middle of the old brickfield, and the two fields in front have been dug for brick earth; the one on the left is now a football field, while the broken ground on the right is covered with beds of nettles, a sure sign of human activities. We follow Sir Thomas Wilson's road which enters a wooded cutting with steep banks on both sides, swings round to the right,

150

and finally emerges between two of the Hampstead Ponds, bringing us back
to South End Green.

Walk Two – The West Heath, Golders Hill Park and the Sandy Heath

Our starting point is Judges' Walk, the mall of Hampstead in the late
eighteenth century. This avenue was probably made earlier in the century
when several others were planted by the owners of large houses near the
Heath, including the Firs Avenue, North End Avenue, and a little-known
lime avenue behind Heath House. When Constable lived nearby in Lower
Terrace he painted many landscapes of the West Heath from this viewpoint
(adding an imaginary windmill in one picture to improve the view). The
hollow below Judges' Walk was one of the largest sandpits on the Heath; it
once contained a pond, the Branch Hill Pond of Constable's pictures, which
later dried up.

The tradition is that Judges' Walk acquired its name during the Great
Plague of 1665, when the judges abandoned London and held the assizes on
the edge of Hampstead Heath. This was regarded merely as legend until the
mid-nineteenth century when it received some unexpected support from Sir
Francis Palgrave, a historian and Deputy Keeper of the Public Records who
lived in Hampstead. He claimed to have found, in a seventeenth-century
law book, confirmation that the assizes were adjourned to Hampstead
because of the sickness raging in London. Unfortunately Palgrave did not
give his source and it has not been found since!

One of the earliest references to Judges' Walk occurs in 1749. At that time
a lawyer named Thomas Clarke, who lived in a house in Branch Hill (later
known as Branch Hill Lodge), leased from the lord of the manor a piece of
ground adjoining his property 'at or near a place called Judges' Bench'.[4]

The earliest form of the name is therefore Judges' Bench, which is even
more intriguing than Judges' Walk, and it can be traced back to the
mid-eighteenth century. (It has been suggested that Judges' Walk may have
taken its name from one of the judges who lived in the vicinity, but there
were none here as early as 1749). Thus the origin of the name remains in
doubt and the local tradition about the plague may not be entirely fanciful;
but it cannot have been the plague of 1665 since no assize was held for
London in that year.

From Judges' Walk we follow the path on the right to the flagstaff. The
original staff was a ship's mast, complete with yard-arm, erected by the lord
of the manor in about 1845, which can be seen in Victorian pictures of the
Heath. The present flagstaff, given by the British Columbia Lumber
Company, was erected in 1954.

This is the summit of the Heath and its history is all around us. It was here
that Sir Thomas Wilson started building his new estate office in 1866, an
action which led to the final battle for the Heath; this is also where the Heath
was dedicated to the people in 1872. The old beacon stood near here in
Tudor times and there is a good view of Shooter's Hill in Kent where there
was another one; for centuries a beacon was lit here to celebrate jubilees and
other national events. The Whitestone Pond itself is an old horse pond

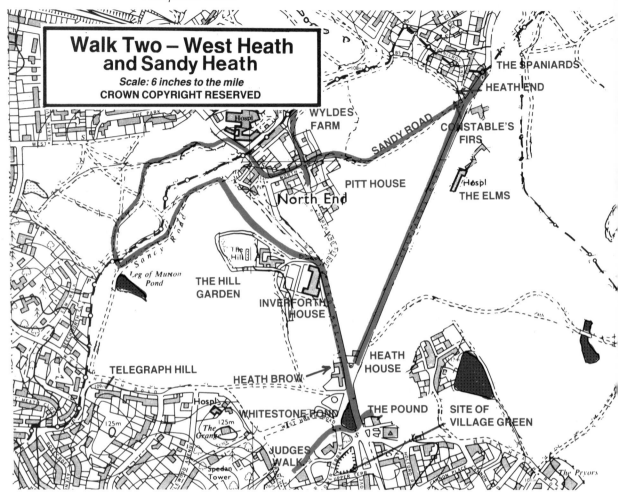

where the animals were watered after the long pull up the hill; it is named after the old milestone which can still be seen in the nearby shrubbery.

A little way to the south, where the covered reservoir now stands between Hampstead Grove and Lower Terrace, lay the old village green. Here the Parliamentary elections for Middlesex were held until 1700, when they were moved to Brentford; the green was later used by the village boys as a cricket ground. On the edge of the green, in what is now the garden of Tudor House, stood the village tree under which George Whitefield preached.

South-east of Whitestone Pond, at the top of East Heath Road, is a large block of flats with a plaque to the author of *The Annals of Hampstead*. Thomas Barratt came to live here in 1877, converting an old house called Bellmoor into a large Victorian mansion. Barratt's life was a Victorian success story in the tradition of Samuel Smiles. As a young man he joined a small soap company, A. & F. Pears, married the boss's daughter, and built it up into a great commercial enterprise, becoming a wealthy man in the process. A brilliant salesman, he was one of the pioneers of modern advertising and made Pears' Soap a household name. His hobby was local history and *The*

88. Whitestone Pond (c.1907).

Annals of Hampstead, published in 1912, is a classic of its kind; as we have seen, he also played a vital part in saving Golders Hill Park and Wyldes Farm for the public.

Next to Bellmoor flats is the Georgian house of Gangmoor, and beyond this a steep pathway leads down to the Vale of Health. On the right of this path is the old village pound, erected in 1787 to replace the earlier one near Jack Straw's Castle; this was where the Heath Keeper locked up the wandering pigs, although he was not allowed to 'pound' the Hampstead donkeys. Barratt adds the curious information that the original side supports of the pound gate were two jaw-bones of a whale.

This part of the Heath was a colourful scene in July 1835 when William IV and Queen Adelaide made their royal visit to Kenwood. Their route was through Hampstead Village and great preparations were made to greet them at the summit of the Heath. A triumphal arch was erected near Whitestone Pond, 'little inferior to Temple-bar in dimensions, and much superior to it in elegance of effect'.[5] It was festooned with branches of trees, flags and ensigns, surmounted by a crown and the initials W.A., and around it was gathered 'all the female beauty of Hampstead'. When the royal party arrived it was greeted with a loyal address by Colonel Bosanquet, the chairman of the reception committee. His Majesty 'appeared much affected by this address' but he made a suitable reply and the royal party went on its way to Kenwood. The only mishap, as the Heath Keeper noted in his diary, was that 'one man lost life at Averstock Hill by coach goin over him'.

North of Whitestone Pond, behind the war memorial, is the eighteenth-century mansion, Heath House. This was the subject of a

153

89. The Triumphal Arch erected in 1835 when William IV visited Kenwood.

delightful and little-known painting by J. Ramsey in 1755 – probably the earliest oil painting of Hampstead (Illustration 12). Heath House was bought in 1790 by Samuel Hoare, the Quaker banker and philanthropist, who lived here until his death in 1825. Hoare was a friend of William Wilberforce and took a leading part in the campaigns to abolish the slave trade and to reform conditions in the prisons; he was also an active member of the local Hampstead community.

Opposite Heath House is Jack Straw's Castle, one of Hampstead's historic inns, where the manor courts used to be held. In the early eighteenth century, when there was a 'horse-course' on the West Heath, the inn was associated with the racing fraternity. It was later a favourite place for Charles Dickens and his friends, who used to have 'a red-hot chop for dinner and a glass of good wine' after a brisk walk across the Heath. Another regular patron was Karl Marx, who lived near Chalk Farm and used to bring his family and friends here after a picnic on the Heath. In the last war the old inn was badly damaged by a parachute mine and it was rebuilt in 1962.

Both the inn and the name have a long history; an alehouse called Jack Straw's Castle is recorded in 1713 and was probably much older, since Tudor brickwork has been found in the foundations of the inn. According to local tradition the site was linked in some way with the Peasants' Revolt of 1381 led by Wat Tyler and Jack Straw. This rising began in Kent and Essex but spread rapidly to other areas, and most of the towns and villages north of London (including St Albans, Barnet, Harrow and Hendon) were affected. It would not be surprising if some of the rebels had camped on Hampstead Heath. On the other hand it has been suggested that Jack Straw was merely a generic name for countrymen, and the 'castle' may have been the ancient earthwork which, it is said, once stood on the crest of the hill.

Beyond Jack Straw's Castle is Heath Brow, where the hamlet of Littleworth once stood. In the last war several large houses were destroyed here at the same time as the old inn. Further along North End way we come to Inverforth House; on this site stood The Hill, a Georgian house where John Gurney Hoare lived during the long struggle for the Heath. This was converted into a large Edwardian mansion by William Lever, the soap millionaire who became Lord Leverhulme; a later owner, Lord Inverforth the shipping magnate, bequeathed it to Manor House Hospital.

Past the house is a lane marked Inverforth Close, near the place where the gibbet once stood; this takes us to The Hill garden, which once belonged to Mrs Lessingham's Heath Lodge. This house was also bought by Lord Leverhulme, who demolished Heath Lodge and made a bridge over the public footpath between his two properties. The Edwardian terraces, gazebos and rose pergola were made by Leverhulme to link the two

90. Jack Straw's Castle (1834).

gardens, one of which (that belonging to the old Heath Lodge) was opened to the public in 1963, while the other is still retained by the hospital.

Not satisfied with the bridge, Lord Leverhulme wanted to acquire the strip of land between his two properties and close the public footpath. In exchange for this he offered The Paddock, a piece of land which he owned on the other side of North End Way, but this proposal was strongly opposed by the Hampstead Heath Protection Society. The matter was still in dispute when Leverhulme died in 1925; at this stage the Society raised the money to buy The Paddock and add it to the Heath.

We leave The Hill garden by the gate, turn left, and almost immediately a rough path forks to the right; this takes us to the Sandy Road, where we turn left and follow the road to the Leg of Mutton Pond. This was made in the winter of 1816, or soon after, as part of a works programme to relieve the parish poor. Originally called the Reservoir, the pond was once a popular bathing place in the summer, causing problems for the Heath Keeper, who wrote in his diary in August 1835, 'Ladys canot pass the Reservoy for men Baything, wishing to ask if to be stoped'.

Across the road is the entrance to Golders Hill Park, once a large private estate landscaped by Humphry Repton. It was put up for auction in 1897, when the last owner died, but was saved from building at the eleventh hour and added to the Heath. The Victorian mansion which replaced the original house was destroyed by a parachute mine in 1941, but the lovely walled garden remains.

Bearing to the right we walk through the park and make for the gate into North End Way, where a right turn brings us to the Old Bull and Bush. According to tradition this was originally a farmhouse and was once the country home of the painter William Hogarth, but there is no evidence to support this. The inn was patronised by Gainsborough, Garrick and Reynolds, and finally achieved fame in Florrie Forde's music-hall song, 'Down at the Old Bull and Bush'. North End was once a little hamlet separated from Hampstead village by the Heath. It was probably the 'Sandgate' referred to in a charter of AD 986 by which the manor of Hampstead was granted to the Abbot of Westminster.

Beyond the Bull and Bush we turn left and soon come to a small crossroads. On our right is North End Avenue, which was part of the ancient road from London to St Albans until the deep cutting of North End Way was made in the early eighteenth century. A little way along, a plaque marks the site of the house where William Pitt, Earl of Chatham, lived for some months in 1767. The statesman, who was going through a nervous breakdown, shut himself up in one room, refusing to see anyone, and had his meals served through a hatch. This mansion, successively known as North End House, Wildwoods and Pitt House, was demolished in 1952, but the large garden became part of the Heath and is now a spectacular wilderness with a ruined classical archway. There is also a fine avenue of limes and chestnuts made in the eighteenth century, which extends across the Heath.

Returning to the crossroads, the country lane on the left leads to Wyldes farmhouse, associated with William Blake and Charles Dickens. The main part of the present farmhouse was probably built in Elizabethan times by

*91. Leg of Mutton Pond
(c.1907).*

Philip Barrett, a tenant farmer. Behind the farmhouse, on the other side of Wildwood Road, lies the Heath Extension which was part of the Wyldes estate and was added to the Heath in 1907.

After this diversion we must again return to the crossroads and take the road straight ahead, which soon turns into a footpath through the wood. This is the so-called Sandy Heath, although most of the sand was carted away by the Midland Railway Company in the 1860s to make their line to St Pancras. We are in fact walking through an enormous sandpit, which accounts for the strange lunar landscape of humps and hollows. The footpath was a public road open to traffic until the early twentieth century; we follow it all the way and just before it comes to an end we can see on our left two great pines, the sole survivors of the Firs Avenue.

The path finally emerges in the eighteenth-century hamlet of Heath End. The most important house here was The Firs, built in 1734 by the retired merchant John Turner, who was either a tobacconist (according to Park) or a linen-draper (according to Barratt). This is the white Georgian house on the left, although it has been much altered and has lost its top storey. John Turner also planted the Firs Avenue and had a hand in making the Sandy Road across the Heath to North End.

The weather-boarded house facing us is Heath End House, once the home of the Arctic explorer Rear-Admiral Sir William Parry, who died in 1855. It was acquired in 1889 by Canon and Mrs Barnett and it was here that Henrietta Barnett planned the campaigns which led to the creation of the Heath Extension and the Hampstead Garden Suburb. A later occupant was the novelist Sir Thomas Hall Caine.

Between Heath End House and the Spaniards Inn is Erskine House; this is on the site of Lord Erskine's house, Evergreen Hill, but only a fragment of the original remains. Thomas Erskine was one of the most successful advocates ever to have practised at the Bar. A prominent Whig, he was a leading opponent of William Pitt's campaign to suppress the radical reform

92. The Old Bull and Bush (c.1790).

movement in the 1790s and successfully defended Thomas Hardy, the secretary of the London Corresponding Society, on a charge of high treason. Erskine also took a keen interest in local affairs and Park's history of Hampstead is dedicated to him.

Beyond Erskine House is the historic Spaniards, the only Hampstead inn to retain its Georgian architecture. The site was once on the boundary between Hampstead Heath and Hornsey Park, belonging to the Bishop of London; it was known as Park Gate and vehicles paid a toll at the old toll house opposite the inn. There are two alternative suggestions as to how the Spaniards got its name. John James Park, the Hampstead historian, says that a house built on the site of the old gatekeeper's lodge was later taken by a Spaniard and converted into a place of entertainment. Alternatively it is said that Count Gondomar, the Spanish ambassador in the reign of James I, took a house here when he retreated from London during a time of plague. There is no evidence to support the Gondomar derivation, which seems unlikely. The Licensing records show a Francis Porero as landlord here in 1721 and he was almost certainly the eponymous Spaniard.

Another puzzle associated with the inn is the location of the Spaniards Pleasure Garden, a popular resort in the middle of the eighteenth century, with an artificial mount used as a viewpoint. According to a contemporary document the landlord of the Spaniards, William Staples, created the garden 'out of a wild and thorny wood full of hills, valleys and sandpits'. An engraving by Chatelain in 1750 (Illustration 11) shows the pleasure garden lying on the southern slope of a small hill. It is difficult to identify this hill, but Christopher Ikin has suggested that it was North Hill which was then

HAMPSTEAD. SPANIARDS ROAD.

*93. The Spaniards Inn
(1838).*

*94. Spaniards Road
(c.1905).*

159

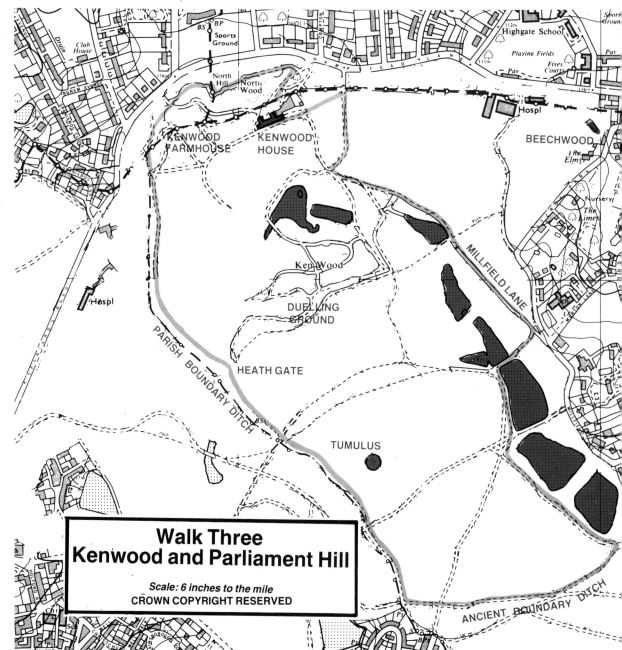

Walk Three
Kenwood and Parliament Hill

Scale: 6 inches to the mile
CROWN COPYRIGHT RESERVED

part of Bishop's Wood and is now in the grounds of Kenwood. North Hill
was in fact called Prospect Hill in the eighteenth century, and there is a large
sandpit on its slopes.

Here we turn back along the Spaniards Road. This is an old track shown in
the 1680 map as 'ye road to Highgate'; it was known as the Broad Walk in
the early nineteenth century when Queen Victoria used to enjoy driving
along it. On the left we pass the holly hedge made by Lord Erskine and then

The Elms, a large Victorian mansion on the site where Mother Huff's once stood, named after a once-famous clump of nine elms.

On both sides of Spaniards Road the sand has been excavated, giving the road the appearance of a causeway. The worst of the digging was in the 1860s but it was going on long before that. In 1823 the author of the *Letters on England, by Victoire, Count de Soligny* (actually written by Peter Patmore) described:

> the sister vales, which sink into the summit of the hill, and are divided from each other by a public road [Spaniards Road] which runs between them in the form of a lofty causeway . . . The soil of these vales consists of a red and yellow sand . . . Any one who pleases is allowed to come here and dig for this sand, and carry it away in any quantity, provided he pays a certain charge to the Lord of the Manor.

Walk Three – Kenwood and Parliament Hill

When Robert Adam was asked to remodel Kenwood in 1764 it was a rambling building made up of a red-brick Queen Anne house with an orangery and various outbuildings. The most important features added by him are the library, one of the finest Adam rooms in existence, and the south front. On the north of the house Adam designed the portico, which sat rather oddly on the earlier building until George Saunders rebuilt the north front in about 1795, replacing the old structure by two projecting wings of white brick.

The interior of Kenwood is rather bare since all the furniture was sold at auction in 1922, but it houses the remarkable picture collection made by Lord Iveagh in the 1880s and 1890s. Rembrandt is represented by a superb self-portrait and Vermeer by the little *Guitar Player*. There is an outstanding collection of Gainsboroughs, including those haughty ladies, Mary, Countess Howe, and Lady Brisco. Reynolds and Romney are perhaps over-represented. The most unusual picture is Claude de Jongh's *Old London Bridge*, an undervalued masterpiece.

Many attempts have been made to explain the origin of Kenwood's name. Daniel Lysons derived it from Reginald de Kentewode, a Dean of St Paul's. The Highgate historian John Lloyd suggested that the Norman bishops of London, who had their hunting lodge at Lodge Hill nearby, named it after Caen in Normandy. Another suggestion was that the stream from which the Highgate Ponds were later formed must have been called the Ken, giving its name to both Kenwood and Kentish Town.

(Overleaf)
95. Highgate Ponds
(T. M. Baynes, 1822).

The earliest references to Kenwood are in the sixteenth century, when it was usually spelt Cane Wood and sometimes Cayne Wood. 'Caen Wood' is not recorded until 1640, while 'Ken Wood' first appears in Rocque's map of London in 1745. The derivation must of course be based on the earliest spelling. Perhaps the most plausible suggestion is that this oak wood took its name from the Anglo-Norman-French word for oak – *keyne*.

We follow the Kenwood terrace to the left, past the attractive service wing built by George Saunders, and go through a gate in the iron fence and up the hill. The brown brick building on the left is the stables built by the second Earl. From the little gazebo there is a superb view across London to the North Downs in the distance. The fields and hedges in the foreground, and

the wooded slope of Highgate on the left, were once part of the Fitzroy Farm estate.

We take the path on the right which leads into Millfield Lane and follow this to the bottom of the hill, where there is a small spring and ornamental fountain erected to the memory of Henry Goodison, treasurer of the campaign to save Kenwood. We soon come to the most unspoilt part of the road, which still gives the impression of a quiet country lane. On the right is the most secluded of the Highgate Ponds, fringed with reeds, and on the left an old hedge studded with gnarled oaks and the rare wild service tree.

Millfield Lane is certainly a sixteenth-century road, but earlier still it may have been part of a medieval way from London to the Bishop's Lodge in Hornsey Park. According to tradition it was along this road that Lieut. William Bygrove led his detachment of light horse to save Kenwood during the Gordon Riots. It was certainly a public road, running into Hampstead Lane, until about 1794 when the second Earl of Mansfield diverted Hampstead Lane to the north and closed the upper part of Millfield Lane to the public; in a map of St Pancras in about 1800 this has become Earl Mansfield's Private Road.

Millfield Lane had its hour of glory in the early nineteenth century. In his autobiography Leigh Hunt, after mentioning its association with Keats, says that 'it has also been paced by Lamb and Hazlitt, and frequented, like the rest of the beautiful neighbourhood, by Coleridge, so that instead of Millfield Lane, which is the name it is known by on earth, it has sometimes been called Poets' Lane'.[6] This was where Coleridge listened to the nightingales, and the upper part is sometimes called Nightingale Lane.

There was a field called Mylfeld in the sixteenth century which must have taken its name from a mill, and one is recorded near here as early as 1335; but was it a windmill or a watermill? The obvious site for a windmill is the crest of Parliament Hill, and there was an earthwork of some kind here as late as the 1880s. Professor Hales thought it was a burial mound but John Lloyd said that 'the inverted bowl-shape of the earthwork, surrounded by a trench, is suggestive of the site of an old windmill'.[7]

More probably, however, the name came from a watermill on the stream in the valley where the Highgate Ponds were later made. In the twelfth century the monk FitzStephen wrote in his *Description of London:* 'to the north lie arable fields, pasture land and lush, level meadows, with brooks flowing amid them, which turn the wheels of watermills with a happy sound'.[8]

In the late eighteenth century, the land on the left of Millfield Lane belonged to Colonel Charles Fitzroy, later Lord Southampton. His Palladian villa, Fitzroy Farm, was roughly where the house called Beechwood now stands, near the top of Fitzroy Park, which was then the carriage drive to Fitzroy Farm. The parkland near the house was landscaped by Capability Brown, and later by Humphry Repton, while the remainder of the 100-acre estate was farmland. The modern house called Fitzroy Farm, opposite the women's swimming pond in Millfield Lane, stands on the site of Lord Southampton's farmhouse and incorporates some of its old beams. The Fitzroy Park estate was sold by the Southampton family in 1840 and several

large villas were built in the grounds.

Millfield Lane is soon joined by Fitzroy Park on the left. This quiet, rural lane will soon be ruined by the development of the land attached to Witanhurst. Leaving Millfield Lane at this junction of roads, we turn right and take the path between two of the Highgate Ponds. The special attraction of these ponds is the water fowl, particularly the great crested grebes which nest here in spring and summer. When the young are first hatched they can be seen riding on their mother's back for a few days; later they are fed with fish by the adult birds until they learn to dive for themselves. Coots, moorhens, mallards, tufted ducks and Canada geese also rear families here and herons can sometimes be seen on the wooded banks.

On the other side of the ponds we turn left and follow the path past the model boating pond, the men's bathing pond, and a third pond. On the far side of this can be seen Millfield Cottage, which once belonged to the Hampstead Water Company but is now much altered. At the end of this pond we take the path on the right which climbs uphill and brings us to a fork. The left-hand path follows an ancient hedge and ditch which once formed the southern boundary of Millfield Farm, and probably also the boundary of William de Blemont's Kenwood estate; but we take the right-hand path instead, up to the windy summit of Parliament Hill with its tremendous panorama of London. As part of the Millfield Farm estate it was advertised for sale and development in 1789 but was fortunately bought by the first Earl of Mansfield; a hundred years later it was added to the Heath.

One suggestion is that the hill got its name because the confederates of Guy Fawkes gathered here in November 1605 to watch the Houses of Parliament being blown up. This is an unlikely story since the conspirators

96. Highgate Model Yacht Club (1854).

165

Hampstead from Parliament Hill

97. *Hampstead from Parliament Hill (c.1906). There were sheep on the Heath as late as 1952.*

were undoubtedly fleeing for their lives at the time. It is true that during the nineteenth century the hill was sometimes called Traitors' Hill, but this was apparently caused by confusion with another hill on the other side of Highgate West Hill. Parliament Hill is probably a more modern name. A survey of Tottenhall manor in 1761 calls it Brockhill, but a map of St Pancras in about 1800 gives the present name: possibly the growth of the legend was the reason for the change.

We follow the path down the other side of the hill until we come to a tall hedge, where we take the path on the right. An old hedge and ditch run parallel to this path on the left, and parish boundary stones, almost buried by the dead leaves in the ditch, mark the old manor and parish boundary between Hampstead and St Pancras. This ditch was described as a 'great ditch' in a document of 1525; it is mentioned three hundred years earlier and may even have been part of a Saxon boundary.

We follow this path until we come to the 'tumulus' on the right and a football field to the left. Here we have a contrast in estate management in the nineteenth century. The fourth Earl of Mansfield owned the land to the right and kept it as farmland. The land on the left, belonging to Sir Thomas Wilson, was exploited as a brickfield, and the soil has been excavated right up to the boundary.

A little further on the ancient ditch reappears among the bushes on the left and we soon come to the western corner of the Kenwood woodland, where the parish boundary is marked by some very old oaks by the ditch.

This area is known as Hampstead Gate and the iron fence marks the boundary of the old Kenwood park. On the right are some giant beeches planted in the eighteenth century, and in spring the ground is carpeted with bluebells. Although the wood itself is only a fragment of that shown on the sixteenth-century map it is still full of interest. In the centre, on the highest ground, is a clearing which legend says is an old duelling ground. This is a good place to watch the woodland birds – great tits, blue-tits, coal-tits, nuthatches, jays and magpies. In the spring you can hear woodpeckers, and kestrels quarter the meadows to the south. There are rabbit burrows in the wood and foxes roam over the Heath at night.

We go through the gate in the iron fence and keep left, still following the old manor and parish boundary which is marked by a wooden paling. The woodland on the left was once part of the garden of The Elms and is well worth exploring; among the overgrown wilderness can be seen the formal terraces, flights of steps and cypresses of a once-beautiful garden.

The paling on the left is soon replaced by woodland and among the trees can be seen a line of old oaks; these again mark the parish boundary and two have stones at their feet. A little further on we leave the path, turn left, and walk across the grass to a five-bar gate and a sunken lane with steep banks: this is the old farm lane which the dairy herd used in moving from Kenwood Farm to the meadows. In the nineteenth century there was a rustic bridge over the muddy lane so that visitors to Kenwood could walk round the park without getting their shoes dirty.

We go through the gate and along the lane. The little group of buildings on the right, originally a cottage, dairy and brewhouse, was built by the second Earl in about 1795. They are described by Sir John Summerson as 'a pretty trio, with stuccoed walls and slate roofs with eaves of exaggerated projection, affecting the Swiss chalet style, whose picturesque virtues had just begun to be appreciated'.[9] The brown brick house ahead of us is all that remains of the octagonal farmhouse built at the same time; the original outline can be traced by a line of brickwork on the ground.

The path on the right takes us to a car park; we cross this and take the little path near the lodge, which climbs up to North Hill and North Wood. These once belonged to Bishop's Wood; they became part of the Kenwood estate when Hampstead Lane was diverted away from the house in the 1790s. The old sandpit on the right suggests that this may have been the 'wild and thorny wood full of hills, valleys and sandpits' where William Staples made the Spaniards Pleasure Garden. Further on we pass the gravestones of two dogs owned by the Grand Duke Michael of Russia, who leased Kenwood from 1909 to 1917. The path finally emerges in the eastern carriage drive which takes us back to Kenwood House.

This is an appropriate place to end our walk, since the saving of Kenwood marked the climax of the long struggle to preserve the Heath and the open spaces around it. However, the battle is by no means over, for the fringes of the Heath are continually under threat from plans for new houses, flats and roads. This unique landscape, preserved for us by the efforts of the Heath defenders in the last one hundred and fifty years, can only be safeguarded for the future by constant vigilance.

[1] Christopher Wade (editor): *More Streets of Hampstead* (1973).

[2] N. Pevsner: *London, except the Cities of London and Westminster* (1952).

[3] *Hampstead and Highgate Express*, 7 February 1920.

[4] Observations for the Hearing, Hoare v Wilson Papers in the Local History Collection of the London Borough of Camden. See also Transactions of the Hampstead Antiquarian and Historical Society, June 1899.

[5] *The Times*, 24 July 1835.

[6] Leigh Hunt: *Autobiography*.

[7] John Henry Lloyd: *History of Highgate* (1888).

[8] FitzStephen's *Description of London* (appended to Stow's *Survey of London*).

Appendix

THE HAMPSTEAD CONTEST

The Hampstead Contest, a Law Case, submitted to counsel, and inscribed to Mrs. L-ss-gh-m. By Farmer Hodge, of Golder's-Green.

APOLLO, *Lessing's* faithful friend,
Who us'd, as poets sing, t'attend
 Her summer months' excursions
Betimes, last spring, was daily seen
At her late cot, on Golder's Green,
 Directing her diversions.

Thence rambling forth round Hampstead Heath,
The finest landskips, heav'n beneath,
 Engaged his roving eyes.
'Here, here, my Lessy, build a cot,
Behold what a delightful spot
 By yonder furze-bush lies.'

Her little poney scarce could make
Its way through bramble, bush and brake,
 To that by Phoebus destin'd;
A spot so snug as if just there
A timorous, trembling, hunted hare,
 Its fluttering form had press'd in 't.

The ground, about, a kind of dale,
The model of an Alpine Vale,
 From wintry storms a shelter:
Unlike the open plain below,
Where whirlwinds from all quarters blow
 Pell-mell and helter-skelter.

Between two hills, a third combin'd
To meet their different slopes, inclin'd
 In waving curves to tally;
Fair opening to the sunny south,
A little westward turn'd its mouth,
 Look'd the sweet-smiling valley.

'Here no bleak winds can break the rest
Of either you or Mrs. B-st,
 Or prattling Polyhymnie![1]
Not blustering Boreas, tho' so rude,
Nor biting Eurus can intrude;
 Unless it's down the chimney.'

Thus saying, without more ado,
Away to Charlton, Phoebus flew,
 And told Sir Thomas W-ls-n:[2]
Of course a grant was made in haste
To Br-dl-y[3] of this piece of waste
 The side of Hampstead hills on.

Meantime fair Lessing turn'd her eyes
And saw, with pleasure and surprize,
 The place was all perfection.
'Be this', she cried, 'Apollo's home,
While here I raise my rustic dome,
 Secure in his protection.'

'Here shall my pretty, prattler play,
Where shines Sol's salutary ray
 In health-diffusing glory:
My growing boy may hence aspire
To emulate his absent sire
 And live in martial story.'

But, lo! no sooner clear'd the ground
Than *some* dull copyholders found,
 His godship had a taste;
On which, they damn'd the Lord, themselves,
And all that were such prudent elves
 To profit by their waste.

Like children, then, who give and take,
They wanted back their bush and brake
 To feed, forsooth, their cattle;
Tho' not a single blade of grass
Or e'en a thistle, for an ass,
 Grew on the field of battle.

Howe'er to work, ding-dong, they went,
Destroy'd the fence, and, not content
 With that, they fir'd a gun off!
Or, as his worship[4], wise as nice,
Says 'two guns once or one gun twice –
 Such mischief! who makes fun of?'

Committed then one bold offender,
Their spades and guns they strait surrender,
 To seek redress at law.
For 'mongst the blacks there was one *White*,[5]
Who, finding he got nothing by 't,
 Sought in the grant a flaw.

'Two acres!' bawl'd he, in a rage,
'And to an actress on the stage,
 A single rood too much is.' –
'Go', Phoebus cried, 'Go, burst with spleen,
Her title's just as good, I ween,
 As that of any Dutchess.'

Hampstead Heath

'Sue, Oafs, for, what you call, your *domage*;
Since by consent of lord and homage,
  Admittance giv'n by Cr-f-rd;[6]
As steward, whether wrong or right,
Let copyholders spit their spite,
  He's bound to furnish law for 't.'

'Yet mind, rash fools, what you're about
Got into law, who'll get you out?
  The Courts love litigation.
Demurrers, issues, judgements, errors,
Will load with costs, and plague with terrours,
  Pregnant procrastination.'

Then, darting an indignant ray,
He told them he'd no more to say,
  They might do as they list;
Vaulted the clouds and left, beneath,
Jack Straw's redoubt[7], with all the heath,
  Envelop'd in a mist.

Say, counsel, learned in the law,
If in the grant you find a flaw;
  Of if your wonted skill
Cannot, tho' such a flaw were plain,
Contrive to stop it up again,
  To save so snug a vill.

For till you, lawyers, touch your fees,
None their possessions hold at ease. –
  Thank heav'n! no grant has Hodge;
Tho' all that he has got, he'd give,
On such a pleasant spot to live
  As *Lessing's* HAMPSTEAD LODGE.

Phoebus Apollo is of course William Addington, who may be the author of the pamphlet. Polyhymnie is the three-year-old son of Addington and Mrs Lessingham.

[1] The names of a little Phoebus and his governess.
[2] The Lord of the manor.
[3] Mrs L's builder.
[4] The worshipful, Mr Justice A—.
[5] A builder, not employed.
[6] The steward of the manor court.
[7] The public-house, on the summit of the hill, called Jack Straw's Castle.

Select Bibliography

Manuscript Sources

(a) The excellent Local History Library of the London Borough of Camden contains, inter alia:

Archives of the Hampstead Heath Protection Society.

Documents in the case of *Hoare v. Wilson*.

The Bellmoor Collection.

The Heal Collection.

Minute Books of the Manor of Hampstead.

Minutes of Hampstead Vestry.

The Feild Booke of 1680.

The Heath Keeper's Diary.

(b) The George Potter Collection and the Crace Collection (British Museum).

(c) 'The Hampstead Contest' (Birmingham Reference Library, LLA 808.81 E/2).

(d) Commons Preservation Society – collection of pamphlets etc, 1829–1901 (G.L.C. History Library).

(e) A plott of the Wodes att Canewood (Public Record Office, MPF 293).

Published Sources

Anon [Thomas Turner], *The Case of Hampstead Heath*, 1857.

Baines, F. E. (ed.), *Records of the Manor, Parish and Borough of Hampstead*, 1890.

Barratt, Thomas J., *The Annals of Hampstead*, 1912.

Barton, Nicholas, *The Lost Rivers of London*, 1962.

Bentwich, Helen, *The Vale of Health*, 1968.

Celoria, F. and Spencer, B. W., 'Eighteenth Century Fieldwork in London and Middlesex; some unpublished drawings by William Stukeley' (*Transactions of London and Middlesex Archaeological Society*, Vol. 22, 1968).

Defoe, Daniel, *A Tour through the Whole Island of Great Britain*, 1724.

Dickinson, H. W., *Water Supply of Greater London*, 1954.

Fitter, R. S. R., *London's Natural History*, 1945.

Gerard, John, *The Herball, or General Historie of Plantes*, 1597.

Gibb, T. E., *A Plea for the Extension of Hampstead Heath*, 1885.

Gilmour, J. S. L. (ed.), *Thomas Johnson: Botanical Journeys in Kent and Hampstead*, 1972.

Girling, M., and Greig, J., 'Palaeoecological investigations of a site at Hampstead Heath' (*Nature*, 7 July 1977).

Goodwin, Thomas, *An Account of the Neutral Saline Waters Recently Discovered at Hampstead*, 1804.

Hampstead Annual, 1897–1906.

Hampstead Heath Extension Committee, *Report*, 1889.

Hampstead Heath Extension Scheme, *Report of the Executive Committee*, 1900.

Hampstead Heath Extension Council, *Report*, 1908.

Hampstead Scientific Society, *Hampstead Heath: Its Geology and Natural History*, 1913.

Hoskins, W. G., and Stamp, L. D., *The Common Lands of England and Wales*, 1963.

Howitt, William, *The Northern Heights of London*, 1869.

Ikin, C. W., *Hampstead Heath Centenary*, 1971.

Ikin, C. W., 'The Battle for the Heath' (*Camden History Review IV*, 1976).

Jackson, A. A., and Croome, D. F., *Rails Through the Clay*, 1962.

Jenkins, S., and Ditchburn, J., *Images of Hampstead*, 1982.

Kennedy, J., *The Manor and Parish Church of Hampstead*, 1906.

Kenwood Preservation Council, *Report*, 1925.

Lee, Charles E., 'Plentyfull Sprynges at Hampstede Hethe' (*Camden History Review III*, 1975).

Lloyd, J. H., *The History, Topography and Antiquities of Highgate*, 1888.

Lloyd, J. H., *Caen Wood and its Associations*, 1892.

London County Council, *Opening of Kenwood by His Majesty the King*, 1925.

London County Council, *Survey of London*, Vols XVII, 1936, and XIX, 1938.

Lorimer, D. H., 'A Mesolithic Site on West Heath, Hampstead' (*London Archaeologist*, Autumn 1976).

Newton, E. E., 'A Few Extracts from the Diary of a Heath Keeper' (*Hampstead Annual*, 1902).

Park, John James, *The Topography and Natural History of Hampstead*, 1814.

Potter, George W., *Hampstead Wells*, 1904.

Potter, George W., *Random Recollections of Hampstead*, 1907.

Prickett, Frederick, *The History and Antiquities of Highgate*, 1842.

Read, Charles H., 'Opening of the Tumulus on Parliament Hill' (*Proceedings of the Society of Antiquaries*, XV, 1894).

Richardson, John, *Highgate*, 1983.

Robbins, Michael, *Middlesex*, 1953.

Scott, Don, *The Nature of Hampstead Heath*, 1979.

Select Committee on Open Spaces (Metropolis), *Report and Evidence*, 1865.

Sexby, J. J., *The Municipal Parks, Gardens and Open Spaces of London*, 1898.

Sharpe, Sutton, 'Hampstead Heath in 1680' (*Hampstead Annual*, 1904–05).

Shaw-Lefevre, G., *English Commons and Forests*, 1894 (revised edition issued as *Commons, Forests and Footpaths*, by Lord Eversley, 1910).

Smith, John G., *History of Charlton*, 1970.

Soame, John, *Hampstead – wells: or, Directions for the Drinking of those Waters*, 1734.

Soligny, Count de (P. G. Patmore), *Letters on England*, 1823.

Stow, John, *A Survey of the Cities of London and Westminster*, 1598.

Sturdy, David, 'Mark of Mellitus' (*Hampstead and Highgate Express*, 10 March 1978).

Sullivan, David, 'Hamlet on the Upgrade' (*Hampstead and Highgate Express*, 25 May 1979).

Summerson, Sir John, *Kenwood*, 1951.

Templewood, Viscount, *The Unbroken Thread*, 1949.

Thompson, F. M. L., *Hampstead: Building a Borough*, 1974.

Transactions of the Hampstead Antiquarian and Historical Society, 1898–1905.

Venning, Philip, 'Sycophant Extraordinary' (*Hampstead and Highgate Express*, 19 May 1978).

Vulliamy, C. E., *The Archaeology of Middlesex*, 1930.

Wade, Christopher (ed.), *The Streets of Hampstead*, 1972.

—— *More Streets of Hampstead*, 1973.

White, Caroline, *Sweet Hampstead*, 1903.

INDEX